PATHWAYS

Listening, Speaking, and Critical Thinking

FOUNDATIONS

Cyndy Fettig   Kathy Najafi   Keith S. Folse, Series Consultant

NATIONAL GEOGRAPHIC LEARNING | HEINLE CENGAGE Learning

Australia • Brazil • Japan • Korea • Mexico • Singapore • Spain • United Kingdom • United States

NATIONAL GEOGRAPHIC LEARNING | HEINLE CENGAGE Learning®

Pathways Foundations
Listening, Speaking, and Critical Thinking
Cyndy Fettig and Kathy Najafi

Publisher: Sherrise Roehr

Executive Editor: Laura Le Dréan

Acquisitions Editor: Tom Jefferies

Development Editor: Jennifer Monaghan

Director of Global Marketing: Ian Martin

Marketing Manager: Emily Stewart

Director of Content and Media Production:
  Michael Burggren

Senior Content Project Manager: Daisy Sosa

Manufacturing Buyer: Marybeth Hennebury

Associate Manager, Operations: Leila Hishmeh

Cover Design: Page 2 LLC

Cover Image: Denis Burdin/Shutterstock

Interior Design: Page 2, LLC

Composition: Page 2, LLC

International Student Edition:

ISBN-13: 978-1-285-17623-9

ISBN-10: 1-285-17623-5

U.S. Edition:

ISBN-13: 978-1-285-17621-5

ISBN-10: 1-285-17621-9

National Geographic Learning
20 Channel Center Street
Boston, MA 02210
USA

Cengage Learning is a leading provider of customized learning solutions with office locations around the globe, including Singapore, the United Kingdom, Australia, Mexico, Brazil, and Japan.

Cengage Learning products are represented in Canada by Nelson Education, Ltd.

Visit National Geographic Learning online at **ngl.cengage.com**

Visit our corporate website at **www.cengage.com**

Printed in the United States of America
2 3 4 5 6 7 8 18 17 16 15 14

The authors and publisher would like to thank the following reviewers:

UNITED STATES **Adrianne Aiko Thompson**, Miami Dade College, Miami, Florida; **Gokhan Alkanat**, Auburn University at Montgomery, Alabama; **Nikki Ashcraft**, Shenandoah University, VA; **Karin Avila-John**, University of Dayton, Ohio; **Shirley Baker**, Alliant International University, California; **John Baker**, Oakland Community College, Michigan; **Evina Baquiran Torres**, Zoni Language Centers, New York; **Michelle Bell**, University of South Florida, Florida; **Nancy Boyer**, Golden West College, California; **Carol Brutza**, Gateway Community College, Connecticut; **Sarah Camp**, University of Kentucky, Center for ESL, Kentucky; **Maria Caratini**, Eastfield College, Texas; **Ana Maria Cepero**, Miami Dade College, Miami, Florida; **Daniel Chaboya**, Tulsa Community College, Oklahoma; **Patricia Chukwueke**, English Language Institute – UCSD Extension, California; **Julia A. Correia**, Henderson State University, Connecticut; **Suzanne Crisci**, Bunker Hill Community College, Massachusetts; **Katie Crowder**, University of North Texas, Texas; **Lynda Dalgish**, Concordia College, New York; Jeffrey Diluglio, Center for English Language and Orientation Programs: Boston University, Massachusetts; **Tim DiMatteo**, Southern New Hampshire University, New Hampshire; **Scott Dirks**, Kaplan International Center at Harvard Square, Massachusetts; **Margo Downey**, Center for English Language and Orientation Programs: Boston University, Massachusetts; **John Drezek**, Richland College, Texas; **Anwar El-Issa**, Antelope Valley College, California; **Anrisa Fannin**, The International Education Center at Diablo Valley College, California; **Jennie Farnell**, University of Connecticut, American Language Program, Connecticut; **Mark Fisher**, Lone Star College, Texas; Celeste Flowers, University of Central Arkansas, Arkansas; John Fox, English Language Institute, Georgia; **Pradel R. Frank**, Miami Dade College, Florida; **Sally Gearheart**, Santa Rosa Jr. College, California; **Karen Grubbs**, ELS Language Centers, Florida; **Joni Hagigeorges**, Salem State University, Massachusetts; **Valerie Heming**, University of Central Missouri, Missouri; **Mary Hill**, North Shore Community College, Massachusetts; **Harry L. Holden**, North Lake College, Texas; **Ingrid Holm**, University of Massachusetts Amherst, Massachusetts; **Marianne Hsu Santelli**, Middlesex County College, New Jersey; **Katie Hurter**, Lone Star College – North Harris, Texas; **Justin Jernigan**, Georgia Gwinnett College, Georgia; **Barbara A. Jonckheere**, American Language Institute at California State University, Long Beach, California; **Susan Jordan**, Fisher College, Massachusetts; **Maria Kasparova**, Bergen Community College, New Jersey; **Gail Kellersberger**, University of Houston-Downtown, Texas; **Christina Kelso**, Austin Peay State University, Tennessee; **Daryl Kinney**, Los Angeles City College, California; **Leslie Kosel Eckstein**, Hillsborough Community College, Florida; **Beth Kozbial Ernst**, University of Wisconsin-Eau Claire, Wisconsin; **Jennifer Lacroix**, Center for English Language and Orientation Programs: Boston University, Massachusetts; **Stuart Landers**, Missouri State University, Missouri; **Margaret V. Layton**, University of Nevada, Reno Intensive English Language Center, Nevada; **Heidi Lieb**, Bergen Community College, New Jersey; **Kerry Linder**, Language Studies International New York, New York; **Jenifer Lucas-Uygun**, Passaic County Community College, New Jersey; **Alison MacAdams**, Approach International Student Center, Massachusetts; **Craig Machado**, Norwalk Community College, Connecticut; **Andrew J. MacNeill**, Southwestern College, California; **Melanie A. Majeski**, Naugatuck Valley Community College, Connecticut; **Wendy Maloney**, College of DuPage, Illinois; **Chris Mares**, University of Maine – Intensive English Institute, Maine; **Josefina Mark**, Union County College, New Jersey; **Connie Mathews**, Nashville State Community College, Tennessee; Bette Matthews, Mid-Pacific Institute, Hawaii; **Marla McDaniels Heath**, Norwalk Community College, Connecticut; **Kimberly McGrath Moreira**, University of Miami, Florida; **Sara McKinnon**, College of Marin, California; **Christine Mekkaoui**, Pittsburg State University, Kansas; **Holly A. Milkowart**, Johnson County Community College, Kansas; **Warren Mosher**, University of Miami, Florida; **Lukas Murphy**, Westchester Community College, New York; **Elena Nehrebecki**, Hudson Community College, New Jersey; **Bjarne Nielsen**, Central Piedmont Community College, North Carolina; **David Nippoldt**, Reedley College, California; **Lucia Parsley**, Virginia Commonwealth University, Virginia; **Wendy Patriquin**, Parkland College, Illinois; **Marion Piccolomini**, Communicate With Ease, LTD, Pennsylvania; **Carolyn Prager**, Spanish-American Institute, New York; **Eileen Prince**, Prince Language Associates Incorporated, Massachusetts; **Sema Pulak**, Texas A & M University, Texas; **James T. Raby**, Clark University, Massachusetts; **Anouchka Rachelson**, Miami-Dade College, Florida; **Lynn Ramage Schaefer**, University of Central Arkansas, Arkansas; **Sherry Rasmussen**, DePaul University, Illinois; **Amy Renehan**, University of Washington, Washington; **Esther Robbins**, Prince George's Community College, Pennsylvania; **Helen Roland**, Miami Dade College, Florida; **Linda Roth**, Vanderbilt University English Language Center, Tennessee; **Janine Rudnick**, El Paso Community College, Texas; **Rita Rutkowski Weber**, University of Wisconsin – Milwaukee, Wisconsin; **Elena Sapp**, INTO Oregon State University, Oregon; **Margaret Shippey**, Miami Dade College, Florida; **Lisa Sieg**, Murray State University, Kentucky; **Alison Stamps**, ESL Center at Mississippi State University, Mississippi; **Peggy Street**, ELS Language Centers, Miami, Florida; **Lydia Streiter**, York College Adult Learning Center, New York; **Nicholas Taggart**, Arkansas State University, Arkansas; **Marcia Takacs**, Coastline Community College, California; **Tamara Teffeteller**, University of California Los Angeles, American Language Center, California; **Rebecca Toner**, English Language Programs, University of Pennsylvania, Pennsylvania; **William G. Trudeau**, Missouri Southern State University, Missouri; **Troy Tucker**, Edison State College, Florida; **Maria Vargas-O'Neel**, Miami Dade College, Florida; **Amerca Vazquez**, Miami Dade College, Florida; **Alison Vinande**, Modesto Junior College, California; **Christie Ward**, Intensive English Language Program, Central Connecticut State University, Connecticut; **Colin S. Ward**, Lone Star College-North Harris, Texas; **Denise L. Warner**, Lansing Community College, Michigan; **Wendy Wish-Bogue**, Valencia Community College, Florida; **Cissy Wong**, Sacramento City College, California; **Kimberly Yoder**, Kent State University, ESL Center, Ohio.

ASIA **Teoh Swee Ai**, Universiti Teknologi Mara, Malaysia; **Nor Azni Abdullah**, Universiti Teknologi Mara, Malaysia; Thomas E. Bieri, Nagoya College, Japan; **Paul Bournhonesque**, Seoul National University of Technology, Korea; **Michael C. Cheng**, National Chengchi University, Taiwan; **Fu-Dong Chiou**, National Taiwan University, Taiwan; **Derek Currie**, Korea University, Sejong Institute of Foreign Language Studies, Korea; **Christoph A. Hafner**, City University of Hong Kong, Hong Kong; **Wenhua Hsu**, I-Shou University, Taiwan; **Helen Huntley**, Hanoi University, Vietnam; **Rob Higgens**, Ritsumeikan University, Japan; **Shih Fan Kao**, JinWen University of Science and Technology, Taiwan; **Ikuko Kashiwabara**, Osaka Electro-Communication University, Japan; **Richard S. Lavin**, Prefecturla University of Kumamoto, Japan; **Mike Lay**, American Institute, Cambodia; **Byoung-Kyo Lee**, Yonsei University, Korea; **Lin Li**, Capital Normal University, China; **Hudson Murrell**, Baiko Gakuin University, Japan; **Keiichi Narita**, Niigata University, Japan; **Huynh Thi Ai Nguyen**, Vietnam USA Society, Vietnam; **James Pham**, IDP Phnom Penh, Cambodia; **Duncan Rose**, British Council, Singapore; **Simone Samuels**, The Indonesia Australia Language Foundation Jakarta, Indonesia; **Wang Songmei**, Beijing Institute of Education Faculty, China; **Chien-Wen Jenny Tseng**, National Sun Yat-Sen University, Taiwan; **Hajime Uematsu**, Hirosaki University, Japan

AUSTRALIA **Susan Austin**, University of South Australia, **Joanne Cummins**, Swinburne College; **Pamela Humphreys**, Griffith University LATIN AMERICA AND THE CARIBBEAN Ramon Aguilar, Universidad Tecnológica de Hermosillo, México; **Livia de Araujo Donnini Rodrigues**, University of São Paolo, Brazil; **Cecilia Avila**, Universidad de Xapala, México; **Beth Bartlett**, Centro Cultural Colombo Americano, Cali, Colombia; **Raúl Billini**, Colegio Loyola, Dominican Republic; **Nohora Edith Bryan**, Universidad de La Sabana, Colombia; **Raquel Hernández Cantú**, Instituto Tecnológico de Monterrey, Mexico; **Millie Commander**, Inter American University of Puerto Rico, Puerto Rico; **Edwin Marín-Arroyo**, Instituto Tecnológico de Costa Rica; **Rosario Mena**, Instituto Cultural Dominico-Americano, Dominican Republic; **Elizabeth Ortiz Lozada**, COPEI-COPOL English Institute, Ecuador; **Gilberto Rios Zamora**, Sinaloa State Language Center, Mexico; **Patricia Veciños**, El Instituto Cultural Argentino Norteamericano, Argentina

MIDDLE EAST AND NORTH AFRICA **Tom Farkas**, American University of Cairo, Egypt; **Ghada Hozayen**, Arab Academy for Science, Technology and Maritime Transport, Egypt; **Jodi Lefort**, Sultan Qaboos University, Muscat, Oman; **Barbara R. Reimer**, CERTESL, UAE University, UAE

Scope and Sequence

Unit	Academic Pathways	Vocabulary	Listening Skills
1 **Same and Different** *Page 1* **Academic Track:** Sociology/Anthropology	**Lesson A:** Listening to a Lecture Conducting a Survey **Lesson B:** Listening to a Conversation Giving a Presentation about Yourself	Understanding meaning from context Using a dictionary to understand new vocabulary Using new vocabulary to complete a conversation Using new vocabulary to describe yourself and others Using new vocabulary to ask and answer questions	Listening to check predictions Listening for main ideas Listening for details Using visuals to understand a listening passage **Pronunciation:** Word stress
2 **Taking Risks** *Page 21* **Academic Track:** Psychology/Sociology	**Lesson A:** Listening to a Radio Show Discussing a Plan **Lesson B:** Listening to a Conversation Giving a Group Presentation	Understanding meaning from context Using a dictionary to understand new vocabulary Using new vocabulary to ask and answer questions	Listening to check predictions Listening for main ideas Listening for details **Pronunciation:** The third person singular
3 **Enjoy the Ride!** *Page 41* **Academic Track:** Interdisciplinary	**Lesson A:** Listening to an Interview Choosing the Best Idea **Lesson B:** Listening to a Conversation Giving a Group Presentation	Using a dictionary to understand new vocabulary Understanding meaning from context Using new vocabulary to complete a conversation Using new vocabulary to ask and answer questions	Listening for order Listening for main ideas Listening for details Using visuals to activate prior knowledge **Pronunciation:** Blended sounds of *There is/There are*
4 **Unusual Destinations** *Page 61* **Academic Track:** Interdisciplinary	**Lesson A:** Listening to a Presentation Choosing the Best Vacation **Lesson B:** Listening to a Group Conversation Giving an Individual Presentation	Using a dictionary to understand new vocabulary Understanding meaning from context Using new vocabulary to complete a conversation Using new vocabulary to ask and answer questions	Using visuals to activate prior knowledge Listening for main ideas Listening for details Listening to check predictions **Pronunciation:** Reduction of *-ing*

Grammar	Speaking Skills	Viewing	Critical Thinking Skills
The simple present and the simple past tense of the verb *be* *Wh-* questions with the verb *be*	Making small talk Conducting a survey Comparing and contrasting yourself to others Describing yourself **Student to Student:** Getting someone's attention **Presentation Skills:** Making eye contact	**Video:** *Coming of Age* Viewing to check predictions Viewing for specific information Relating video to personal experiences and opinions	Reflecting on identity Comparing similarities and differences Considering possible solutions Using a pie chart to organize notes for a presentation **Critical Thinking Focus:** Reflecting
The simple present tense The simple present tense with *Wh-* questions	Discussing activities and risks Discussing a plan Asking questions in a conversation Discussing survey results Showing interest **Student to Student:** Making eye contact **Presentation Skills:** Asking for questions	**Video:** *Highlining Yosemite Falls* Activating prior knowledge Viewing to check predictions Viewing for specific information	Identifying risks Making a plan and setting goals Ranking information in order of importance Evaluating risks people take **Critical Thinking Focus:** Making predictions
There is, there are, there was, there were *Like to, want to, need to*	Asking questions to encourage communication Evaluating options Explaining steps in a process Offering encouragement **Student to Student:** Saying thanks **Presentation Skills:** Introducing your group	**Video:** *Indian Railways* Activating prior knowledge Viewing to check predictions Viewing for specific information	Ranking information in order of safety Identifying steps in a process Stating pros and cons Understanding information in a graph Explaining information in a graph Using a chart to categorize Making inferences **Critical Thinking Focus:** Listening for order
The present continuous The present continuous in questions	Talking about what you are doing Asking for repetition Performing a role play Explaining preferences **Student to Student:** Working together **Presentation Skills:** Using graphics	**Video:** *Blue Lagoon* Activating prior knowledge Viewing to check predictions Viewing for specific information	Understanding visuals Reflecting on ideas about travel Interpreting a poem Using a chart to categorize information Making inferences Collaborating Considering pros and cons Completing a pie chart **Critical Thinking Focus:** Describing

Unit	Academic Pathways	Vocabulary	Listening Skills
5 **Our Changing World** *Page 81* Academic Track: Interdisciplinary	**Lesson A:** Listening to a Lecture Discussing Traditions **Lesson B:** Listening to a Short Documentary Presenting to a Small Group	Using a dictionary to understand new vocabulary Understanding meaning from context Using new vocabulary to complete a conversation Using new vocabulary to complete a text	Listening for main ideas Listening for details Listening to check predictions **Pronunciation:** Using intonation to ask for something or make a request The intonation of *Wh-* questions
6 **Facing Challenges** *Page 101* Academic Track: Interdisciplinary	**Lesson A:** Listening to a Presentation Talking about the Past **Lesson B:** Listening to a Conversation Presenting from Notes	Using a dictionary to understand new vocabulary Understanding meaning from context Using new vocabulary to complete a conversation Using new vocabulary to complete a text Using new vocabulary to discuss the unit theme	Listening to check predictions Listening for main ideas Listening for details **Pronunciation:** The simple past tense *-ed* endings
7 **Lost and Found** *Page 121* Academic Track: History/ Anthropology/ Archaeology	**Lesson A:** Listening to a Guided Tour Talking about the Past **Lesson B:** Listening to a Conversation Role-Playing	Using a dictionary to understand new vocabulary Understanding meaning from context Using new vocabulary to complete a conversation Using new vocabulary to complete a text	Listening for main ideas Listening for details Listening for emphasized words Listening to check predictions Note-taking while listening **Pronunciation:** Word stress
8 **A New View** *Page 141* Academic Track: Science/ Technology	**Lesson A:** Listening to a Scientific Talk Conducting a Survey **Lesson B:** Listening to a Debate between Friends Participating in a Debate	Understanding meaning from context Using new vocabulary to complete an article Using new vocabulary to discuss the unit theme	Listening for main ideas Listening for details Listening for statements of opinion Listening to check predictions **Pronunciation:** Contractions with *will*

Grammar	Speaking Skills	Viewing	Critical Thinking Skills
The simple past tense The simple present vs. the simple past tense of the verb *be*	Using past tense expressions Discussing traditions Asking for something/Making a request **Student to Student:** Asking questions **Presentation Skills:** Presenting to a small group	**Video:** *Pow-wows* Viewing for specific information Relating video to personal experiences and opinions	Evaluating the pros and cons of a changing world Using a chart to organize information Relating your own background to others **Critical Thinking Focus:** Listening for the main idea
Irregular past tense verbs The simple past tense	Expressing difficulty with something Talking about challenges Talking about the past Discussing challenging careers **Student to Student:** Taking turns **Presentation Skills:** Presenting to a group using notes	**Video:** *Antarctic Challenge* Viewing for specific information Relating video to personal experiences and opinions	Making inferences Making comparisons Relating information from discussions to personal experience **Critical Thinking Focus:** Making inferences
Informational past tense questions The conjunction *because*	Asking informational questions Expressing past facts and generalizations with *used to* Asking and answering questions with *because* **Student to Student:** Asking for clarification **Presentation Skills:** Using body language	**Video:** *The Lost World of Angkor* Understanding visuals Activating prior knowledge Viewing for numbers Viewing for specific information Discussing the video as it relates to today's cities	Understanding information on a time line Making inferences Reflecting on your own culture's history **Critical Thinking Focus:** Recalling facts
The future with *will* The future with *be going to*	Describing objects using adjectives Talking about the future Conducting a survey **Student to Student:** Showing agreement and disagreement **Presentation Skills:** Debating	**Video:** *Augmented Reality* Viewing to check predictions Viewing for specific information	Using a chart to categorize information Evaluating the pros and cons of a topic **Critical Thinking Focus:** Discussing pros and cons

Each unit consists of two lessons which include the following sections:

- Building Vocabulary
- Using Vocabulary
- Developing Listening Skills
- Exploring Spoken English
- Speaking (called "Engage" in Lesson B)

An **academic pathway** is clearly labeled for learners, starting with formal listening (e.g., lectures) and moving to a more informal context (e.g., a conversation between students in a study group).

The **"Exploring the Theme"** section provides a visual introduction to the unit and encourages learners to think critically and share ideas about the unit topic.

UNIT **4**

Unusual Destinations

ACADEMIC PATHWAYS
Lesson A: Listening to a Presentation
            Choosing the Best Vacation
Lesson B: Listening to a Group Conversation
            Giving an Individual Presentation

Think and Discuss

1. Do you know what these lights are in the sky?
2. Where can you see these lights?
3. What do you think the unit is about?

▲ Northern lights in the night sky over Norway

61

Exploring the Theme: Unusual Destinations

Look at the photos and read the captions and the information. Then discuss the questions.

1. Where do you like to travel?
2. What differences do you see between the photos? How are they alike and how are they different?
3. Look at the two photos. Which place do you want to go to?

Explore the Unusual

Are you bored with the same vacation spot? Our world has so many beautiful places. Some of them are natural like this cave in the Bahamas and some of them are manmade like this cave in Turkey. Many people go to the same place every year. This year, be adventurous and plan your next vacation at an unusual destination. Then, spend the rest of your life enjoying the natural and manmade wonders across our world. So many places and so little time!

▲ A manmade cave in Turkey

▲ A diver explores an underwater cave in the Bahamas

THE PATHWAY TO ACADEMIC SUCCESS...

Key academic and high-frequency vocabulary is introduced, practiced, and expanded throughout each unit. Lessons A and B each present and practice 6 to 8 items.

A **"Developing Listening Skills"** section follows a before, during, and after listening approach to give learners the tools necessary to master listening skills for a variety of contexts.

Listening activities encourage learners to listen for and consolidate key information, reinforcing the language, and allowing learners to think critically about the information they hear.

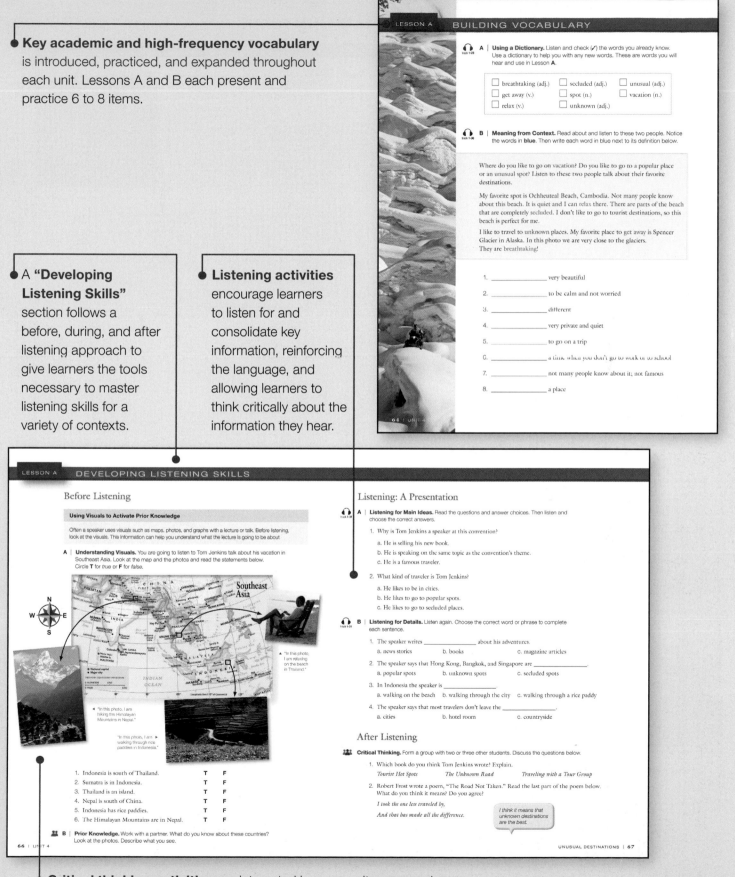

Critical thinking activities are integrated in every unit, encouraging continuous engagement in developing academic skills.

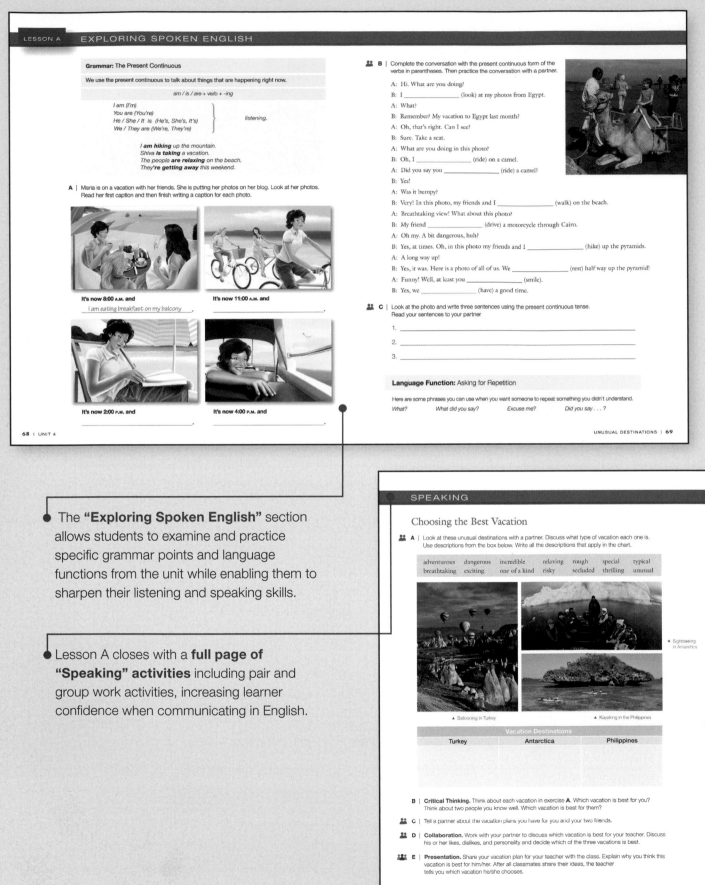

LESSON A   EXPLORING SPOKEN ENGLISH

Grammar: The Present Continuous

We use the present continuous to talk about things that are happening right now.

am / is / are + verb + -ing

I am (I'm)
You are (You're)
He / She / It is (He's, She's, It's)   listening.
We / They are (We're, They're)

I **am hiking** up the mountain.
Shiva **is taking** a vacation.
The people **are relaxing** on the beach.
They**'re getting away** this weekend.

A | Maria is on a vacation with her friends. She is putting her photos on her blog. Look at her photos. Read her first caption and then finish writing a caption for each photo.

It's now 8:00 A.M. and
I am eating breakfast on my balcony .

It's now 11:00 A.M. and
_____ .

It's now 2:00 P.M. and
_____ .

It's now 4:00 P.M. and
_____ .

B | Complete the conversation with the present continuous form of the verbs in parentheses. Then practice the conversation with a partner.

A: Hi. What are you doing?
B: I _____ (look) at my photos from Egypt.
A: What?
B: Remember? My vacation to Egypt last month?
A: Oh, that's right. Can I see?
B: Sure. Take a seat.
A: What are you doing in this photo?
B: Oh, I _____ (ride) on a camel.
A: Did you say you _____ (ride) a camel?
B: Yes!
A: Was it bumpy?
B: Very! In this photo, my friends and I _____ (walk) on the beach.
A: Breathtaking view! What about this photo?
B: My friend _____ (drive) a motorcycle through Cairo.
A: Oh my. A bit dangerous, huh?
B: Yes, at times. Oh, in this photo my friends and I _____ (hike) up the pyramids.
A: A long way up!
B: Yes, it was. Here is a photo of all of us. We _____ (rest) half way up the pyramid!
A: Funny! Well, at least you _____ (smile).
B: Yes, we _____ (have) a good time.

C | Look at the photo and write three sentences using the present continuous tense. Read your sentences to your partner

1. _____
2. _____
3. _____

Language Function: Asking for Repetition

Here are some phrases you can use when you want someone to repeat something you didn't understand.
What?   What did you say?   Excuse me?   Did you say . . . ?

The **"Exploring Spoken English"** section allows students to examine and practice specific grammar points and language functions from the unit while enabling them to sharpen their listening and speaking skills.

Lesson A closes with a **full page of "Speaking" activities** including pair and group work activities, increasing learner confidence when communicating in English.

SPEAKING

Choosing the Best Vacation

A | Look at these unusual destinations with a partner. Discuss what type of vacation each one is. Use descriptions from the box below. Write all the descriptions that apply in the chart.

| adventurous | dangerous | incredible | relaxing | rough | special | typical |
| breathtaking | exciting | one of a kind | risky | secluded | thrilling | unusual |

◄ Sightseeing in Antarctica

▲ Ballooning in Turkey   ▲ Kayaking in the Philippines

Vacation Destinations		
Turkey	Antarctica	Philippines

B | **Critical Thinking.** Think about each vacation in exercise **A**. Which vacation is best for you? Think about two people you know well. Which vacation is best for them?

C | Tell a partner about the vacation plans you have for you and your two friends.

D | **Collaboration.** Work with your partner to discuss which vacation is best for your teacher. Discuss his or her likes, dislikes, and personality and decide which of the three vacations is best.

E | **Presentation.** Share your vacation plan for your teacher with the class. Explain why you think this vacation is best for him/her. After all classmates share their ideas, the teacher tells you which vacation he/she chooses.

● The **"Viewing" section** works as a content-bridge between Lesson A and Lesson B and includes two pages of activities based on a fascinating video from National Geographic.

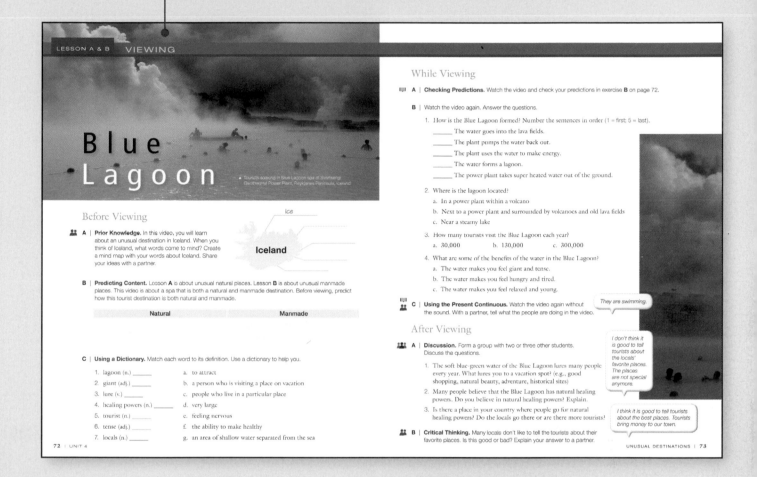

LESSON A & B VIEWING

Blue Lagoon

Tourists soaking in Blue Lagoon spa at Svartsengi Geothermal Power Plant, Reykjanes Peninsula, Iceland

Before Viewing

A | Prior Knowledge. In this video, you will learn about an unusual destination in Iceland. When you think of Iceland, what words come to mind? Create a mind map with your words about Iceland. Share your ideas with a partner.

ice

Iceland

B | Predicting Content. Lesson **A** is about unusual natural places. Lesson **B** is about unusual manmade places. This video is about a spa that is both a natural and manmade destination. Before viewing, predict how this tourist destination is both natural and manmade.

Natural	Manmade

C | Using a Dictionary. Match each word to its definition. Use a dictionary to help you.

1. lagoon (n.) _____   a. to attract
2. giant (adj.) _____   b. a person who is visiting a place on vacation
3. lure (v.) _____   c. people who live in a particular place
4. healing powers (n.) _____   d. very large
5. tourist (n.) _____   e. feeling nervous
6. tense (adj.) _____   f. the ability to make healthy
7. locals (n.) _____   g. an area of shallow water separated from the sea

72 | UNIT 4

While Viewing

A | Checking Predictions. Watch the video and check your predictions in exercise **B** on page 72.

B | Watch the video again. Answer the questions.

1. How is the Blue Lagoon formed? Number the sentences in order (1 = first; 5 = last).
   _____ The water goes into the lava fields.
   _____ The plant pumps the water back out.
   _____ The plant uses the water to make energy.
   _____ The water forms a lagoon.
   _____ The power plant takes super heated water out of the ground.

2. Where is the lagoon located?
   a. In a power plant within a volcano
   b. Next to a power plant and surrounded by volcanoes and old lava fields
   c. Near a steamy lake

3. How many tourists visit the Blue Lagoon each year?
   a. 30,000   b. 130,000   c. 300,000

4. What are some of the benefits of the water in the Blue Lagoon?
   a. The water makes you feel giant and tense.
   b. The water makes you feel hungry and tired.
   c. The water makes you feel relaxed and young.

C | Using the Present Continuous. Watch the video again without the sound. With a partner, tell what the people are doing in the video.

> They are swimming.

After Viewing

A | Discussion. Form a group with two or three other students. Discuss the questions.

1. The soft blue-green water of the Blue Lagoon lures many people every year. What lures you to a vacation spot? (e.g., good shopping, natural beauty, adventure, historical sites)

2. Many people believe that the Blue Lagoon has natural healing powers. Do you believe in natural healing powers? Explain.

3. Is there a place in your country where people go for natural healing powers? Do the locals go there or are there more tourists?

B | Critical Thinking. Many locals don't like to tell the tourists about their favorite places. Is this good or bad? Explain your answer to a partner.

> I don't think it is good to tell tourists about the locals' favorite places. The places are not special anymore.

> I think it is good to tell tourists about the best places. Tourists bring money to our town.

UNUSUAL DESTINATIONS | 73

● **A DVD for each level** contains 10 authentic videos from National Geographic specially adapted for English language learners.

NATIONAL GEOGRAPHIC LEARNING | HEINLE CENGAGE Learning

PATHWAYS Foundations
Listening, Speaking, and Critical Thinking

DVD
Total Running Time: 35:59

© 2012 National Geographic Learning, a part of Cengage Learning. ALL RIGHTS RESERVED.

A variety of activity types simulates the academic classroom where multiple skills must be applied simultaneously for success.

An **"Engage" section** at the end of the unit challenges learners with an end-of-unit presentation project. Speaking tips are offered for formal and informal group communication, instructing students to interact appropriately in different academic situations.

"Presentation Skills" boxes offer helpful tips and suggestions for successful academic presentations.

A 19-page **"Independent Student Handbook"** is conveniently located in the back of the book and provides helpful self-study strategies for students to become better independent learners.

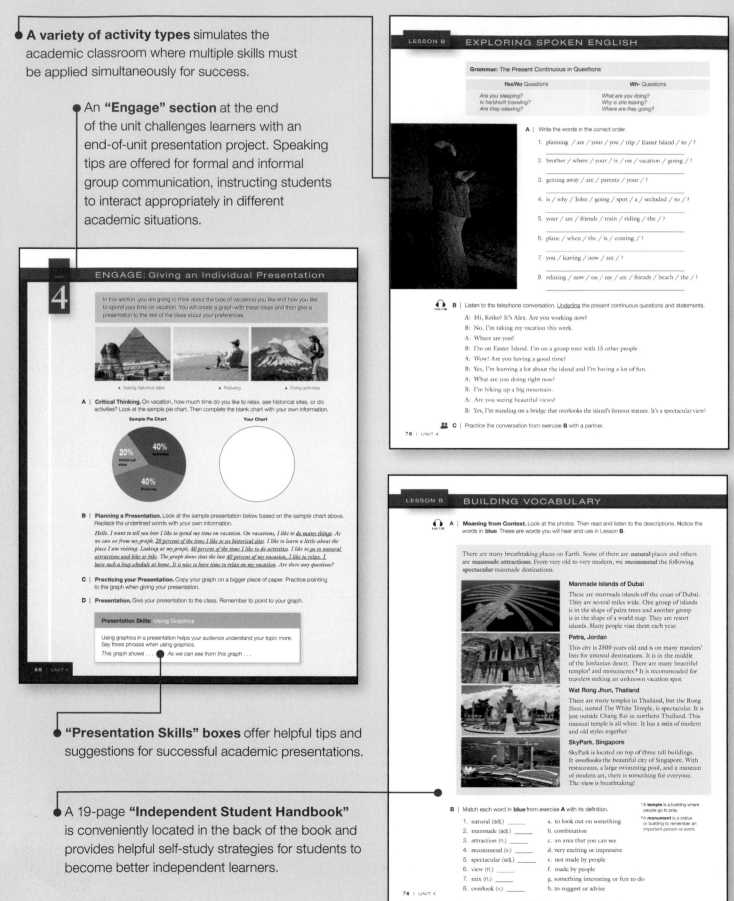

LESSON B — EXPLORING SPOKEN ENGLISH

Grammar: The Present Continuous in Questions

Yes/No Questions	**Wh- Questions**
Are you sleeping?	What are you doing?
Is he/she/it traveling?	Why is she leaving?
Are they relaxing?	Where are they going?

A | Write the words in the correct order.

1. planning / are / your / you / trip / Easter Island / to / ?
   _____
2. brother / where / your / is / on / vacation / going / ?
   _____
3. getting away / are / parents / your / ?
   _____
4. is / why / John / going / spot / a / secluded / to / ?
   _____
5. your / are / friends / train / riding / the / ?
   _____
6. plane / when / the / is / coming / ?
   _____
7. you / leaving / now / are / ?
   _____
8. relaxing / now / on / my / are / friends / beach / the / ?
   _____

B | Listen to the telephone conversation. Underline the present continuous questions and statements.

A: Hi, Keiko? It's Alex. Are you working now?
B: No, I'm taking my vacation this week.
A: Where are you?
B: I'm on Easter Island. I'm on a group tour with 15 other people.
A: Wow! Are you having a good time?
B: Yes, I'm learning a lot about the island and I'm having a lot of fun.
A: What are you doing right now?
B: I'm hiking up a big mountain.
A: Are you seeing beautiful views?
B: Yes, I'm standing on a bridge that overlooks the island's famous statues. It's a spectacular view!

C | Practice the conversation from exercise **B** with a partner.

78 | UNIT 4

UNIT 4 — ENGAGE: Giving an Individual Presentation

In this section, you are going to think about the type of vacations you like and how you like to spend your time on vacation. You will create a graph with these ideas and then give a presentation to the rest of the class about your preferences.

▲ Seeing historical sites   ▲ Relaxing   ▲ Doing activities

A | **Critical Thinking.** On vacation, how much time do you like to relax, see historical sites, or do activities? Look at the sample pie chart. Then complete the blank chart with your own information.

Sample Pie Chart

- 40% Activities
- 40% Relaxing
- 20% Historical sites

Your Chart

B | **Planning a Presentation.** Look at the sample presentation below based on the sample chart above. Replace the underlined words with your own information.

Hello. I want to tell you how I like to spend my time on vacation. On vacations, I like to do many things. As we can see from my graph, 20 percent of the time I like to see historical sites. I like to learn a little about the place I am visiting. Looking at my graph, 40 percent of the time I like to do activities. I like to go to natural attractions and hike or bike. The graph shows that the last 40 percent of my vacation, I like to relax. I have such a busy schedule at home. It is nice to have time to relax on my vacation. Are there any questions?

C | **Practicing your Presentation.** Copy your graph on a bigger piece of paper. Practice pointing to the graph when giving your presentation.

D | **Presentation.** Give your presentation to the class. Remember to point to your graph.

> **Presentation Skills:** Using Graphics
>
> Using graphics in a presentation helps your audience understand your topic more. Say these phrases when using graphics.
> *This graph shows . . .   As we can see from this graph . . .*

80 | UNIT 4

LESSON B — BUILDING VOCABULARY

A | **Meaning from Context.** Look at the photos. Then read and listen to the descriptions. Notice the words in blue. These are words you will hear and use in Lesson **B**.

There are many breathtaking places on Earth. Some of them are **natural** places and others are **manmade attractions**. From very old to very modern, we **recommend** the following **spectacular** manmade destinations.

Manmade islands of Dubai

These are manmade islands off the coast of Dubai. They are several miles wide. One group of islands is in the shape of palm trees and another group is in the shape of a world map. They are resort islands. Many people visit them each year.

Petra, Jordan

This city is 2500 years old and is on many travelers' lists for unusual destinations. It is in the middle of the Jordanian desert. There are many beautiful temples[1] and monuments.[2] It is recommended for travelers seeking an unknown vacation spot.

Wat Rong Jhun, Thailand

There are many temples in Thailand, but the Rong Jhun, named The White Temple, is spectacular. It is just outside Chang Rai in northern Thailand. This unusual temple is all white. It has a **mix** of modern and old styles together.

SkyPark, Singapore

SkyPark is located on top of three tall buildings. It **overlooks** the beautiful city of Singapore. With restaurants, a large swimming pool, and a museum of modern art, there is something for everyone. The **view** is breathtaking!

[1] A **temple** is a building where people go to pray.
[2] A **monument** is a statue or building to remember an important person or event.

B | Match each word in blue from exercise **A** with its definition.

1. natural (adj.) _____   a. to look out on something
2. manmade (adj.) _____   b. combination
3. attraction (n.) _____   c. an area that you can see
4. recommend (v.) _____   d. very exciting or impressive
5. spectacular (adj.) _____ e. not made by people
6. view (n.) _____   f. made by people
7. mix (n.) _____   g. something interesting or fun to do
8. overlook (v.) _____   h. to suggest or advise

74 | UNIT 4

For the Teacher:

Perfect for integrating language practice with exciting visuals, **video clips from National Geographic** bring the sights and sounds of our world into the classroom.

A **Teacher's Guide** is available in an easy-to-use format and includes teacher's notes, expansion activities, and answer keys for activities in the student book.

The Assessment CD-ROM with Exam*View*® is a test-generating software program with a data bank of ready-made questions designed to allow teachers to assess students quickly and effectively.

Bringing a new dimension to the language learning classroom, the **Classroom Presentation Tool CD-ROM** makes instruction clearer and learning easier through interactive activities, audio and video clips, and Presentation Worksheets.

For the Student:

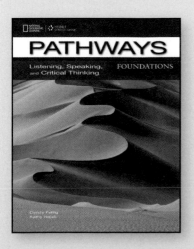

The **Student Book** helps students achieve academic success in and outside of the classroom.

Audio CDs contain the audio recordings for the exercises in the student books.

 Powered by MyELT, the **Online Workbook** has both teacher-led and self-study options. It contains 8 National Geographic video clips, supported by interactive, automatically graded activities that practice the skills learned in the student books.

Visit elt.heinle.com/pathways for additional teacher and student resources.

Credits

Photo Images

Cover and i: Dennis Burdin/Shutterstock, **iv:** Alison Wright/National Geographic, **iv:** Mikey Schaefer/National Geographic, **iv:** Eldad Carin/iStockphoto.com, **iv:** Wes C. Skiles/National Geographic, **vi:** Fritz Hoffmann/National Geographic, **vi:** Tojy George/National Geographic My Shot/National Geographic, **vi:** Kenneth Garrett/National Geographic, **vi:** Christian Darkin/Alamy, **1:** Stuart McClymont/Getty Images, **2:** Asiaselects/Alamy, **3:** Dmitry Kalinovsky/Shutterstock.com, **3**: Creatas/Jupiter Images, **4:** StockLite/Shutterstock.com, **4:** East/Shutterstock.com, **5:** Lisa Davis/iStockphoto.com, **6:** Elena Zidkova/Shutterstock.com, **8:** Sam Edwards/Alamy, **10:** Edyta Pawlowska/Shutterstock.com, **10:** Jupiterimages/Brand X Pictures/Jupiter Images, **10:** Design Pics Inc./Alamy, **12:** Lynn Johnson/National Geographic, **13:** Photo Mere Travel/Alamy, **14:** Prof. Stan Z. Li and his research team of the Center for Biometrics and Security Research, **15:** Randy Olson/National Geographic, **16:** Ariwasabi/Shutterstock.com, **16:** Ariwasabi/Shutterstock.com, **18:** Alison Wright/National Geographic, **21:** Brian J. Skerry/National Geographic, **22:** biletskiy/Shutterstock.com, **22:** Maxim Blinkov/Shutterstock, **22:** Erik Isakson/Jupiter Images, **22–23:** Mikey Schaefer/National Geographic, **24:** Rich Reid/National Geographic, **25:** Skip Brown/National Geographic, **26:** Bobby Model/National Geographic, **26:** ImagesBazaar/Getty Images, **28:** Paul Chesley/National Geographic, **28:** Quincy Dein/Shutterstock.com, **28:** Marcin Balcerzak/Shutterstock, **28:** Andrei Zarubaika/Shutterstock.com, **28:** John Burcham/National Geographic, **28:** Tim Laman/National Geographic, **29:** Brian J. Skerry/National Geographic, **30:** Quincy Dein/Shutterstock.com, **30:** Subbotina Anna/Shutterstock.com, **30:** Kate Thompson/National Geographic, **30:** Paul Chesley/National Geographic, **30:** Skip Brown/National Geographic, **30:** John Burcham/National Geographic, **30:** Tim Laman/National Geographic, **30:** Ipatov 2010/used under license by www.shutterstock.com, **31:** Skip Brown/National Geographic, **32:** Jimmy Chin/National Geographic, **33:** Jimmy Chin/National Geographic, **34:** David Doubilet/National Geographic, **36:** John Goodrich/www.zenfolio.com\tiger372, **37:** B. Anthony Stewart/National Geographic, **38:** Bill Hatcher/National Geographic, **39:** John Burcham/National Geographic, **40:** Kate Thompson/National Geographic, **41:** Justin Guariglia/National Geographic, **42:** Beverly Joubert/National Geographic, **42–43:** Eldad Carin/iStockphoto.com, **43:** Steve Raymer/National Geographic, **43:** Christopher Pillitz/Photonica World/Getty Images, **44:** Tang Chhin SOTHY/AFP/Getty Images/Newscom, **44:** Scott Dalton/The New York Times/Redux Pictures, **44:** Justin Guariglia/National Geographic, **45:** bubamarac/Shutterstock.com, **47:** Cameron Lawson/National Geographic, **49:** Scott S. Warren/National Geographic, **51:** Chris Howes/Wild Places Photography/Alamy, **51:** Glowimages RM/Alamy, **51:** oksana.perkins/Shutterstock.com, **51:** Pagina/Shutterstock.com, **52:** dbimages/Alamy, **52:** david pearson/Alamy, **54:** Simon Holdcroft/Alamy, **54:** Hung Chung Chih/Shutterstock.com, **54:** ATS Ltd/BWP Media/Getty Images, **56:** Chris Turner/Shutterstock.com, **56:** Stuart Pearce/Age Fotostock, **58:** George Dolgikh/Shutterstock.com, **58:** Suzi Nelson/Shutterstock, **58:** kaczor58/Shutterstock.com, **58:** Li Chaoshu/Shutterstock.com, **58:** bogdan ionescu/Shutterstock.com, **61:** Roy Samuelsen/National Geographic My Shot/National Geographic, **62–63:** Wes C. Skiles/National Geographic, **63:** Tracing Tea/Shutterstock.com, **64:** Alaska Stock Images/Glow Images, **65:** William Berry/Shutterstock.com **66:** Scott S. Warren/National Geographic, **66:** Justin Guariglia/National Geographic, **66:** lina aidukaite/Alamy, **69:** Tino Soriano/National Geographic, **71:** Kani Polat/National Geographic, **71:** Jason Edwards/National Geographic, **71:** Edwin Verin/Shutterstock.com, **72:** Sisse Brimberg/National Geographic, **73:** Keenpress/National Geographic, **74:** National Geographic Image Collection/Alamy Limited, **74:** Yory Frenklakh/Shutterstock.com, **74:** zirconicusso/Shutterstock.com, **74:** pkphotos.com/Alamy, **75:** TonyV3112/Shutterstock.com, **76:** Alison Wright/National Geographic, **78:** Randall J. Olson/National Geographic, **80:** N Mrtgh/Shutterstock.com, **80:** Creatas/Thinkstock, **80:** Sergiy Zavgorodny/Shutterstock.com, **81:** Fritz Hoffmann/National Geographic, **82–83:** Markley Boyer/National Geographic, **82–83:** Cameron Davidson/Corbis, **84:** Fritz Hoffmann/National Geographic, **85:** Fritz Hoffmann/National Geographic, **86:** Paul Chesley/National Geographic,

continued on p. 178

Same and Different

ACADEMIC PATHWAYS

Lesson A: Listening to a Lecture
Conducting a Survey
Lesson B: Listening to a Conversation
Giving a Presentation about Yourself

Think and Discuss

1. Look at the two children. How are they the same?
2. Do you know any twins? How are they different?
3. In what ways are all people the same?

Look at the map and photos and read the information. Then discuss the questions.

1. How is this map different from other maps?
2. Which countries have the most people?
3. Look at the families. What do you know about their countries?
4. How are you the same as and different from these people?

▲ A family in China

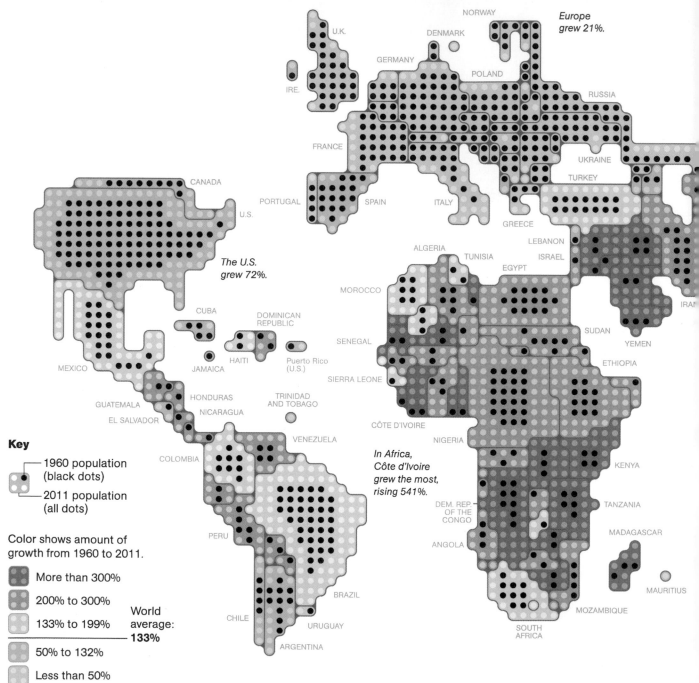

Europe grew 21%.

The U.S. grew 72%.

In Africa, Côte d'Ivoire grew the most, rising 541%.

Key

— 1960 population (black dots)
— 2011 population (all dots)

Color shows amount of growth from 1960 to 2011.

More than 300%
200% to 300%
133% to 199%   World average: **133%**
50% to 132%
Less than 50%

▲ A family in India   ▲ A family in Venezuela

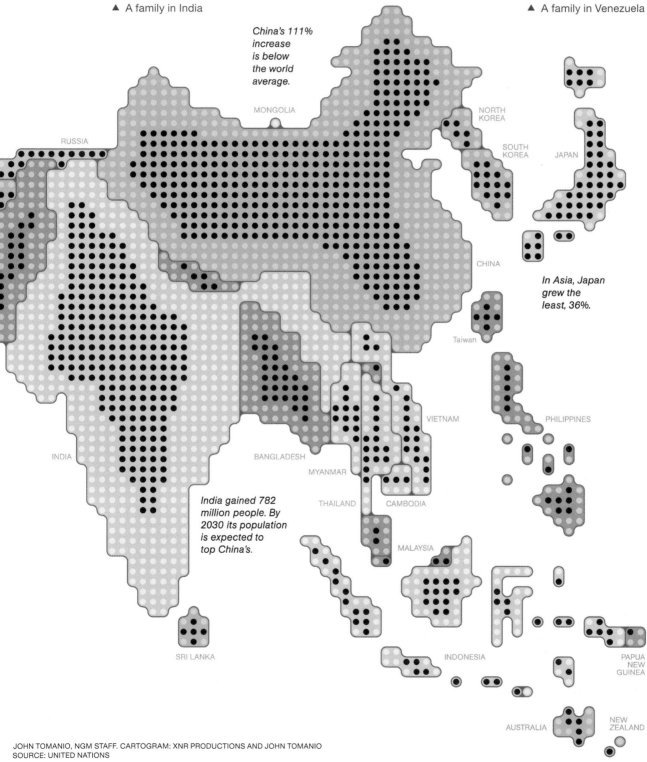

China's 111% increase is below the world average.

MONGOLIA

RUSSIA

NORTH KOREA

SOUTH KOREA

JAPAN

CHINA

In Asia, Japan grew the least, 36%.

Taiwan

VIETNAM

PHILIPPINES

BANGLADESH

MYANMAR

India gained 782 million people. By 2030 its population is expected to top China's.

THAILAND

CAMBODIA

MALAYSIA

INDIA

SRI LANKA

INDONESIA

PAPUA NEW GUINEA

AUSTRALIA

NEW ZEALAND

JOHN TOMANIO, NGM STAFF. CARTOGRAM: XNR PRODUCTIONS AND JOHN TOMANIO
SOURCE: UNITED NATIONS

A | Listen and check (✓) the words you already know. These are words you will hear and use in Lesson **A**.

track 1-01

- ☐ athlete (n.)
- ☐ be a native of (v.)
- ☐ carefree (adj.)
- ☐ foreign (adj.)
- ☐ home country (n.)
- ☐ international (adj.)
- ☐ outgoing (adj.)
- ☐ traveler (n.)

B | **Meaning from Context.** Read and listen to the article. Notice the words in **blue**.

track 1-02

Where are you from? For third culture kids, that is a hard question. Third culture kids don't live in their **home country**. They live in many countries. Third culture kids are the same as and different from other kids. Listen to their stories.

Marisa

Hi, I am Marisa. I am a third culture kid. I **am a native of** the United States, but the United States is not my home country. My home countries are Singapore, the Philippines, and Korea. I am a world **traveler** and I speak many languages. I am the same as and different from other American kids. I like music and movies like other American kids. But I like **international** music and **foreign** movies instead of pop music and Hollywood movies.

Hello. I am Toshio. I am a third culture kid, too. I am a native of Japan, but Japan is not my home country. My home countries are South Africa and Zimbabwe. I am the same as and different from other Japanese kids. I like sports and I am an **athlete** like many Japanese boys my age. I play cricket[1] but many Japanese boys play baseball. I am **carefree** and **outgoing**.

Toshio

[1] **Cricket** is a game played by two teams using a ball, a bat, and a set of sticks.

C | **Using a Dictionary.** Match each word in **blue** from exercise **B** with its definition. Use your dictionary to help you.

1. carefree ___f___
2. home country _____
3. international _____
4. foreign _____
5. traveler _____
6. outgoing _____
7. athlete _____
8. be a native of _____

a. the country where you were born
b. wanting to meet and talk to new people
c. not from your own country
d. be born in a particular place
e. someone who is good at sports
f. without any problems or worries
g. having to do with more than one nation
h. someone who visits other cities and countries

A | Work with a partner. Read the conversation and fill in each blank with a word from the box. Then practice the conversation.

| athlete | foreign | home country | international | ~~a native of~~ | traveler |

A: Hi! What's your name?

B: My name is Thomas.

A: Where are you from?

B: I am (1) __a native of__ Australia, but Australia is not my (2) _____ . I live in many (3) _____ countries.

A: Are you a world (4) _____ ?

B: Kind of. I am a third culture kid.

A: What is that?

B: A person who is (5) _____ , who lives in many countries but never their own home country.

A: Interesting! Are you the same as other kids?

B: Yes, I like sports, such as soccer and volleyball.

A: Oh, I am an (6) _____ , too.

B: Do you play cricket?

A: Is that the same as baseball?

B: Yes, it's similar. Some things are the same and some things are different.

B | **Discussion.** With your partner, discuss the questions below.

1. What is your home country? How is your home country the same as or different from other countries?

2. What do kids like to do for fun in your country?

3. Are you a traveler? Do you travel to foreign countries? Where do you go?

4. Do you like sports? Are you an athlete? Which sports do you play or watch?

▲ Cricket is a popular sport in the United Kingdom and Australia.

track 1-03

Pronunciation: Word Stress

Speakers stress certain words when they compare and contrast. The words **and**, **but**, and **both** are often stressed.

Example: *I have a twin sister. We are the same **and** we are different. We are **both** athletes. She likes to play tennis **but** I like to play soccer. We **both** like music. She likes pop music **but** I like rock music.*

track 1-04

A | Read and listen to the description. Then listen and notice the extra stress on the underlined words *and, but,* and *both.*

My twin brother and I are the same <u>and</u> we are different. We are from New Zealand. I live in my home country, <u>but</u> my twin lives in Ireland. We are <u>both</u> travelers. I like to visit places near my house, <u>but</u> my brother likes to travel to foreign countries. We are <u>both</u> big eaters. I like to eat meat, <u>but</u> he is a vegetarian. We <u>both</u> like to watch movies. I like to watch dramas, <u>but</u> he likes to watch action movies. We are <u>both</u> married. I have kids, <u>but</u> he doesn't have kids, yet. We are the same <u>and</u> we are different!

Use *both* when something is true about two people or things.

Examples:
We <u>are both</u> tall.
We <u>both like</u> soccer.

B | With a partner, write five things that are the same and different about both of you. Practice reading the sentences. Emphasize the words *and, but,* and *both.*

Example: I am an athlete *and* my partner is an athlete.
I am a traveler, *but* my partner is not a traveler.
We are *both* outgoing.

Before Listening

A | **Using a Dictionary.** You will hear these words in the lecture. Work with a partner and check (✓) the words you already know. Use a dictionary to help you with any words you don't know.

☐ adopt (v.)   ☐ identical (adj.)   ☐ shy (adj.)   ☐ similar (adj.)   ☐ nervous (adj.)

B | Write each word from exercise **A** next to its definition below.

1. _____similar_____ almost the same but not exactly the same
2. _____shy_____ not confident to talk to people
3. _____nervous_____ worried and frightened
4. _____adopt_____ to legally make someone else's child part of your family
5. _____identical_____ exactly the same

C | Predicting Content. You are going to listen to a lecture about identical twins. With a partner, check (✓) the topics you think you will hear about.

☐ Why twins are the same ☐ Why twins are different ☐ How twins are made

✓☐ Stories about twins ☐ Favorite foods of twins ☐ Families of twins

Listening: A Lecture

A | Checking Predictions. Listen to the lecture. Then look at your predictions from exercise **C**. Which predictions were correct?

Track 1-05

B | Listening for the Main Idea. Listen to the lecture again. Check (✓) the main idea of the lecture.

Track 1-05

☐ Identical twins come from the same egg that split into two.

✓☐ Some identical twins are similar and some are very different.

☐ Identical twins are very rare.

☐ It is best for identical twins to grow up in different families.

C | Listening for Details. Listen to the lecture again. The teacher mentions the "Jim Twins." <u>Underline</u> the facts the teacher mentions.

Track 1-05

✓1. The two boys lived with different families.

2. They both were five feet tall.

3. Their wives were named Linda and Betty.

4. They both were firefighters.

5. They both liked sports.

6. ✗They both had cats named Toy.

7. ✓They both had sons named James Alan.

8. ✓They are 39 years old now.

After Listening

Survey. Choose a word from the box below. Think of a question and survey your classmates. Write a statement about your results and then read your statement to the class.

athlete	native of	outgoing	traveler
carefree	nervous	shy	twin

Example: Five people in the class are shy.

Are you shy?

Yes, I am shy.

Language Function: Making Small Talk

Small talk is a short, informal conversation about common interests. Small talk is a good way to begin talking to someone. Some general topics include nationality, occupation, hobbies, and the weather. Here are some questions you can use to begin small talk.

Where are you from?   *What do you do?*   *What are your hobbies?*   *It's cold today, isn't it?*

A | Read and listen to the conversations. Then underline the phrases the speakers use to make small talk.

track **1-06**

Conversation 1

A: Where are you from?

B: I'm from Brazil.
   Where are you from?

A: I'm from Japan.
   What do you do?

B: I am a student.
   What do you do?

A: I am a writer.

B: It's nice to meet you.

A: Nice to meet you, too.

Conversation 2

A: It's cold today, isn't it?.

B: Yes! The weather is very different from yesterday.

A: Yes. Yesterday was so hot!

B: I know. And, today it is freezing. Very strange!

A: I agree.

B | Which topics do they talk about in exercise **A**?

C | Practice the conversations from exercise **A** with a partner. Then switch roles and practice them again.

Grammar: The Simple Present and the Simple Past Tense of the Verb *Be*

The Simple Present Tense of the Verb *Be*

Affirmative Statements (+)	Negative Statements (-)	Questions (?)
I **am** an athlete. I**'m** an athlete.	I **am not** an athlete. I**'m not** an athlete.	**Am** I an athlete?
You **are** a native. You**'re** a native.	You **are not** a native. You**'re not** a native.	**Are** you a native?
He **is** a traveler. He**'s** a traveler.	He **is not** a traveler. He**'s not** a traveler.	**Is** he a traveler?
We **are** twins. We**'re** twins.	We **are not** twins. We**'re not** twins.	**Are** we twins?
They **are** third culture kids. They**'re** third culture kids.	They **are not** third culture kids. They**'re not** third culture kids.	**Are** they third culture kids?

The Simple Past Tense of the Verb *Be*

Affirmative Statements (+)	Negative Statements (-)	Questions (?)
I **was** shy.	I **was not** shy.	**Was** I shy?
You **were** different.	You **were not** different.	**Were** you different?
She **was** nervous.	She **was not** nervous.	**Was** she nervous?
We **were** carefree.	We **were not** carefree.	**Were** we carefree?
They **were** foreign.	They **were not** foreign.	**Were** they foreign?

A | Listen to the conversation. Fill in the blanks with the form of *be* you hear. Check your answers with a partner. Then practice the conversation.

(ck 1-07)

A: Hi, I (1) ____am____ Tanya. What's your name?

B: My name (2) ____is____ Anna. Where (3) ____are____ you from?

A: I (4) ____was____ born in Costa Rica, but I live in Russia. My mother (5) ~~is~~ come ____ from Costa Rica, but my dad (6) ~~is~~ come. ____ from Russia. Where (7) ____are____ you from?

B: We (8) ____are____ from Canada. It (9) ____is____ a nice place to live.

A: (10) ~~Were~~ ~~Did~~ ____ you born in Canada?

B: I (11) ____was____ born in Canada, but my parents (12) ____~~are~~ were____ born in Sweden.

B | Use exercise **A** as a model for your own conversation about you and your family. Practice with your partner.

SAME AND DIFFERENT | **9**

C | Tony is a third culture kid. He has many friends. Here is his blog. Complete his sentences with the simple present or simple past of the verb *be*. Use the negative when you see the symbol (-). Compare your answers with your partner.

Welcome to Tony's page

Hi! I (1) _____am_____ Tony. I live in Italy. I (2) _____wasn't_____ born in the United States, but I (3) _____am_____ (-) really American.

I (4) _____am_____ a third culture kid.

Photos of Friends/Places

This (5) _____is_____ my friend Cleo. She (6) _____is_____ from Italy. She (7) _____is_____ very outgoing. She (8) _____is_____ (-) a third culture kid.

This (9) _____is_____ my friend Carlos. Carlos' home country (10) _____is_____ Argentina. He (11) _____is_____ a third culture kid, too. He (12) _____was_____ shy in the beginning, but now he (13) _____is_____ very outgoing. We (14) _____are_____ both travelers. We go on many trips together. Last month we (15) _____were_____ in Switzerland. In this photo Carlos (16) _____was_____ on top of a mountain in the Alps. It (17) _____was_____ a difficult climb. We (18) _____were_____ tired, but we (19) _____were_____ happy we made it to the top!

D | **Self-Reflection.** How were you as a child? How are you different today? Look at the example. Then complete your own chart.

Child	Now
I was very shy.	I am outgoing.
I wasn't an athlete.	I am an athlete.
I was not carefree.	I am carefree.

Child	Now

E | **Follow-Up.** Tell the class how you are different now. Read your sentences aloud.

Conducting a Survey

A | Complete the survey with your own answers. Then ask a partner the questions. Write your partner's answers in the chart.

General Questions	You	Your Partner
1. How old are you?	I'm 27 y/old	He is 20 y/old.
2. Where are you from?	I'm from Mongolia	He's from Vietnam
3. What do you do?	I am a student	He is a student
4. What are your hobbies?	I like photography's.	He likes watching movie

Personality Questions

	You	Your Partner
1. Are you carefree or nervous?	Yes, I'am	Yes, He is
2. Are you shy or outgoing?	Yes, I'am	Yes, He is
3. Are you a traveler or a homebody (someone who likes to stay at home)?	I'm a homebody	He is a traveler
4. Are you an athlete or a non-athlete?	I'm not an athlete	He isn't an athlete.

B | **Pair Work.** How are you the same as and different from your partner? Look at the sample diagram. Then complete the Venn diagram with your partner's and your information.

I am from China.

I'm from M
I like photography

Roberto is from Italy.

He is from V

He likes watching movie

We both like sports.

We are both shy and nervous. We aren't an athlete

C | **Presentation.** Form a group with two or three other students. Tell your group how you and your partner are the same and how you are different.

Coming of Age

◀ Fulani boys take their cows to find food during the wet season. If they are successful, the boys become men.

Before Viewing

A | Critical Thinking. This video is a "coming of age" story. "Coming of age" is a young person's change from a child to an adult. When and how this happens is different in each country. Read about some customs below. What do you think are the reasons for these customs? Work with a partner to complete the chart.

People	Custom	Reasons
Australian Aborigines	Teenage boys live alone in the wilderness for six months.	
Latin America	15-year-old girls have a party called a *Quinceañera*. First they go to church and then they have a big party.	

B | Predicting Content. In the video, you will learn about a boy named Yoro from Africa. Yoro makes a trip with his cows to prove that he is a man. How is your life the same as Yoro's? How is your life different? Complete the diagram.

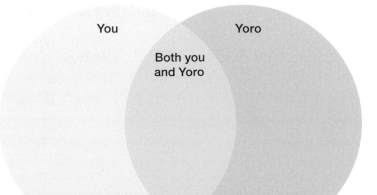

You

Yoro

Both you and Yoro

C | Using a Dictionary. Match each word to its definition. Use a dictionary to help you.

1. become an adult (v.) ___d___   a. a long trip

2. journey (n.) ___a___   b. feel uneasy or anxious

3. take care of (v.) ___e___   c. have ceremonies, parties, and other festivities

4. worry (v.) ___b___   d. turn into a fully grown person

5. celebrate (v.) ___c___   e. watch over

While Viewing

A | Watch the video. Add any new information to the diagram in exercise **B** on page 12.

B | Read the statements. Then watch the video again and circle **T** for *true* or **F** for *false*.

1. Yoro walked for three months.	T	F
2. The boys take the journey to find water for their cows.	T	F
3. Girls take the journey also.	T	F
4. The boys have little food on their journey and only drink milk.	T	F
5. If the cows are OK, then Yoro will be a man.	T	F

After Viewing

A | Critical Thinking. Read the reasons for some coming of age customs. Form a group with two or three other students. Discuss the reasons. Do you agree?

Custom	Reason	Your Belief
Cutting boys' skin to make it look like a crocodile.	To become a man, a boy has to experience pain. He will remember the pain later and it will help him face his troubles in the future.	
Parents choose the person their child can marry.	The parents believe they can make a better choice.	

B | Discussion. With a partner, discuss the questions below.

1. Does your country or your family celebrate coming of age? Is it the same for boys and girls?

2. What did you do when you became an adult?

> *In my country, we become an adult when we are 20. We have a big party.*

BUILDING VOCABULARY

A | Listen and check (✓) the words you already know. These are words you will hear and use in Lesson **B**

track 1-08

- [ ] alike (adj.)
- [ ] billion (n.)
- [ ] Earth (n.)
- [ ] female (n.)
- [ ] male (n.)
- [ ] one of a kind (adj.)
- [ ] special (adj.)
- [ ] typical (adj.)

B | **Meaning from Context.** Read and listen to the presentation. Notice the words in **blue**.

track 1-09

The world now has seven **billion** people. How are you and these seven billion others **alike**? Are you the same? Or are you **one of a kind**? Are you **special**? Within the seven billion people on **Earth**, who is the **typical** person? Listen to the facts about Earth's seven billion people.

A typical person . . .

makes less than $12,000 USD a year.

is a male.   has a cell phone.

is right-handed.   doesn't have a car.

does not have a bank account.   is 28 years old.

▲ The typical person is a 28-year-old Han Chinese man. There are over 9,000,000 Han Chinese males in the world.

Typical means different things in every country. A typical person in your home country is different from a typical person in another country. For example, a typical male in Holland is 5'11", but a typical male in Peru is 5'4". A typical Japanese female lives to be 86 years old, but a typical woman from Afghanistan lives to be 45 years old. A typical American uses 100 gallons of water a day at home, but a typical Ethiopian uses 2.5 gallons of water a day. Typical is different for each country.

C | Write each word in **blue** from exercise **B** next to its definition.

1. _female_ (n.) a woman
2. _billion_ (n.) a number (1,000,000,000)
3. _one of a kind_ (adj.) different from everyone else
4. _male_ (n.) a man

5. _special_ (adj.) different from what is usual
6. _typical_ (adj.) having the usual features or qualities of a group
7. _earth_ (n.) our planet
8. _alike_ (adj.) in a similar way; almost exactly the same

USING VOCABULARY

A | Read the sentences. Circle the correct word.

1. There are over seven billion people on (Earth / alike).

2. Some people have (typical / special) talents, such as singing or juggling.

3. There are more (males / females) on Earth.

4. She is not like anyone I know. She is (alike / one of a kind).

5. It is (typical / alike) to have many males on a soccer team.

6. Identical twins are very much (one of a kind / alike).

7. Seven (billion / special) people is a lot for our planet's resources.

8. Typical Japanese (females / males) live to be 86 years old.

Critical Thinking Focus

Reflecting
Discussions and debates are a large part of class. Reflecting or thinking about what you believe in before a discussion can help you communicate your ideas better during class.

B | **Discussion.** With a partner, discuss the question.

How are you the same as and how are you different from the typical person described in exercise **B** on page 14?

C | **Critical Thinking.** With a group, think about the students in your class. How are you the same? Complete the sentences below. Share your ideas with the rest of the class.

Example: _____ A typical student in this class takes the bus to school. _____.

1. A typical student in this class _____.

2. A typical student in this class _____.

3. A typical student in this class _____.

Before Listening

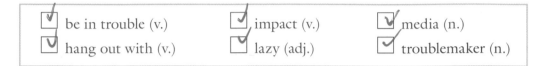

A | **Using a Dictionary.** Listen and check (✓) the words you already know. You will hear these words in the conversation. Use a dictionary to help you with any new words.

track 1-10

✓ be in trouble (v.)	✓ impact (v.)	✓ media (n.)
✓ hang out with (v.)	☐ lazy (adj.)	✓ troublemaker (n.)

B | Write each word from exercise **A** next to its definition below.

1. _____media_____ television, radio, and newspapers

2. __troublemaker__ someone who causes problems

3. _be in trouble_ to be in a difficult situation

4. _____Lazy_____ not doing work

5. _hang out with_ to spend a lot of time with

6. ____impact____ to change someone or something

C | **Understanding Visuals.** Look at the photos and read the captions. Then discuss the questions with a partner.

1. Who is the person in the photos?

2. How is she different in the two photos?

3. Why do you think she is sad now?

▲ Carmen, February 2012   ▲ Carmen, November 2012

Listening: A Conversation

A | Critical Thinking. Listen to the conversation. What is the best way for Kathryn to talk to her sister Carmen about her problem? Circle your choice. Discuss your choice with a partner.

1. Tell her parents about the situation first. Then talk to Carmen together with their parents.

2. Don't talk with Carmen. Ignore her and hopefully she will change.

3. Be friends with Brian, too. Hang out with them so she can impact them.

B | Listening for Details. Listen to the conversation again. Write the words from the box in the chart below.

– bad student	good listener	great sister	hard worker	– not happy
good girl	good student	–hard time	– lazy	– troublemaker

Carmen Before	Carmen Now
good student	

After Listening

A | Follow-Up. Use the information from the chart in exercise **B** above. Write three sentences using the verb *be*.

Example: _Carmen was a good student._

1. _____

2. _____

3. _____

B | Discussion. Form a group of three or four other students. Discuss the following questions.

1. Who is your best friend? Describe him/her.

2. How do your friends impact you?

3. Who do you hang out with on the weekends? What do you do?

4. Is anyone lazy in your family? Is anyone a troublemaker in your family? Explain.

5. Do you watch television? Do you surf the Internet often? How does the media impact you?

Grammar: *Wh-* Questions with the Verb *Be*

We use *what, where, when, why,* and *how* with the verb *be* to find out more information.

Examples:

Who	**Who are** you? **Who is** typical? **Who are** they? **Who was** that? **Who was** there?
What	**What is** his name? **What are** they? **What was** it? **What were** they?
Where	**Where am** I? **Where is** it? **Where is** he from? **Where are** they? **Where were** you?
Why	**Why am** I here? **Why are** you nervous? **Why was** she there? **Why were** you happy?
How	**How are** you? **How is** she? **How was** the game?

A | Write the words in the correct order to form *Wh-* questions.

1. they / who / are ?

   Who are they?

2. from / you / where / are / ?

   Where are you from?

3. nervous / why / she / was / ?

   Why was she nervous?

4. country / you / what / from / are / ?

   What are you from?

5. were / the / how / twins / different / ?

   How twins were different?

6. his / who / twin / is / brother / ?

   Who is his twin brother!

B | Read the scenarios. Write two *Wh-* questions with the verb *be*.

Scenario #1: Your friend was not it class for a week.

   Where was your friend?

Scenario #2: My friend is a troublemaker.

   Why is your friend is troublemaker?
   is

C | Complete the conversation with the *Wh-* questions.

How is he?	What was the movie about?	Why are you tired?
Who is the actor?	Where were you last night?	Who was there?

A: Hi. _Where were you last night?_

B: I was at the movies.

A: _Who was there?_

B: Sam and I were there together.

A: _How is he?_

B: He is good.

A: _What was the movie about?_

B: It was about a teenager. He was sad but he changed. In the end, he was happy.

A: _Who is the actor?_

B: I don't remember his name. I'm tired. I'm going to bed.

A: _Why are you tired?_

B: It is late! Good night!

D | Work with a partner. Practice the conversation in exercise **C**. Then switch roles and practice it again.

E | Form a group with two or three other students. Use the words in the box and other words to describe typical people in your country.

carefree	hardworking	lazy	outgoing	nervous	troublemaker

Typical baby _trouble maker_

Typical teenager _outgoing, nervous,_

Typical mother _hardworking_

Typical father _carefree_

Student to Student

Getting Someone's Attention

To talk to someone, you need to get their attention first. Say *Excuse me*, and then ask them a question to begin your conversation.

In this section, you will give a presentation about yourself. Who are you and how did you become that way? What impacts your life?

A | Self-Reflection. These things impact who you are: family, friends, media, experiences. What percentage do they impact your life? Is there anything else that impacts you? Look at the sample pie chart and then fill in your own pie chart.

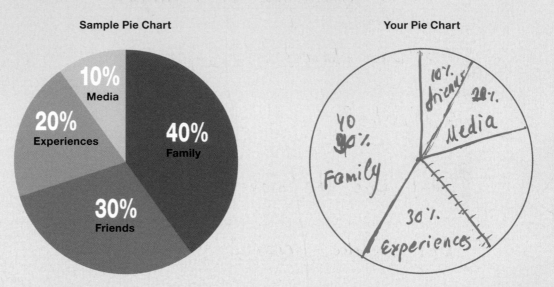

Sample Pie Chart

Your Pie Chart

B | Planning a Presentation. Look at the sample presentation below based on the sample pie chart above. Use the sample to help you write your own presentation.

There are many things that impact people's lives. Parents, friends, experiences, and the media all make us who we are. As you can see from my chart, my parents impact my life the most. They are hardworking and I am hardworking because of them. My friends also impact my life. I spend a lot of time with them and we do many things together. I travel a little and I learn from my experiences. These experiences also impact my life. I don't watch a lot of TV so the media doesn't change my life very much.

Presentation Skills: Making Eye Contact

Looking at the audience is very important. Using eye contact shows that you are excited to give a presentation. Also, making eye contact with your audience will help engage your audience. They will listen more.

C | Practice Your Presentation. Practice reading your presentation. Remember to make eye contact.

D | Presentation. Give your presentation to the class. Remember to look at your audience. Show your chart to the class as you speak.

Taking Risks

ACADEMIC PATHWAYS
Lesson A: Listening to a Radio Show
              Discussing a Plan
Lesson B: Listening to a Conversation
              Giving a Group Presentation

Think and Discuss

1. Look at the photo and read the caption. What is this person doing?
2. Does this look like fun? Why, or why not?

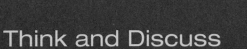
▲ An oceanic whitetip shark swims past a diver.

21

Exploring the Theme: Taking Risks

Look at the photos and read the captions and the information.
Then discuss the questions.

1. Which of the people in these photos is taking the biggest risk?

2. What are two reasons people risk their lives doing sports?

3. What are some risks people take in their everyday lives?

4. Do you like to take risks? Why, or why not?

snowboarding ▶

8.4
MILLION
PEOPLE*

6.8
MILLION
PEOPLE*

◀ skateboarding

kickboxing ▶

4.8
MILLION
PEOPLE*

Source: SGMA, 2008
* Number of people who do
these sports in the U.S.

Explorer Jimmy Chin climbing in
Yosemite National Park, U.S.

A | Listen and check (✓) the words you already know. These are words you will hear and use in Lesson **A**.

track 1-12

- ☐ adventure (n.)
- ☐ danger (n.)
- ☐ exciting (adj.)
- ☐ extreme (adj.)
- ☐ popular (adj.)
- ☐ risky (adj.)
- ☐ seek (v.)
- ☐ thrill (n.)

B | **Meaning from Context.** Read and listen to the article. Notice the words in **blue**.

track 1-13

Adventure trips are very **popular** now. More and more people want to do something different and exciting on vacation. Some people **seek danger** and some people get a thrill from adventure. These people often choose an **extreme** vacation. They parachute, cliff jump, and dive with sharks. Some people want a less **risky** adventure. They hike, raft, and cycle. There is an adventure for everyone and they are all **exciting**! Listen to Jane talk about the kinds of adventure trips she goes on.

A small tour boat gets close to the glaciers in Alaska.

C | **Using a Dictionary.** Match each word in **blue** from exercise **B** with its definition. Use your dictionary to help you.

1. risky ___h___
2. thrill ___d___
3. exciting ___f___
4. extreme ___g___
5. danger ___c___
6. seek ___b___
7. popular ___a___
8. adventure ___e___

a. liked by a lot of people
b. to try to find or do something
c. not safe
d. strong excitement and pleasure
e. an unusual experience
f. making you feel happy or interested
g. beyond the normal, very dangerous or difficult
h. something that may harm you

"I go on an adventure trip every year. I walk through the African Safari and I bike through the Grand Canyon. This is a photo from my favorite adventure trip in Alaska. We take a small boat and get very close to the glaciers. They are beautiful."

A | Complete each sentence with a word from exercise **A** on page 24.

(Thrill seekers)

1. Swimming with sharks is very __dangerous__. They might bite you.

2. My brothers always __seek__ adventure. They try to find exciting things to do.

3. Adventure trips are becoming more ~~extreme~~ *exciting popular*. Many people are doing them.

4. I love scuba diving! It is so ~~risky popular~~. ~~extreme~~. ~~risky~~ *exciting*

5. Parachuting, cliff jumping, and highlining are

    __extreme__ sports.

6. We want to do something different. We want to go on

    an __adventure__.

7. Risk takers like the __thrill__ of
   the adventure.

8. If you want a sport with ~~risky~~ *extreme risk*, try
   cliff jumping. It is one sport where you need to be
   very careful.

B | **Discussion.** With a partner, discuss the
questions below.

1. Which **extreme** sports are **popular** in your country?
   Why do you think they are popular?

2. What activities give you a **thrill**?

3. What kind of **adventure** do you like? An adventure
   in a city or in nature?

4. What do you **seek** in a trip?

5. What **dangers** are around you?

Cars and buses in my city are dangerous!

Swimming in the ocean gives me a thrill.

I seek peace and quiet in a trip.

Before Listening

A | **Using a Dictionary.** You will listen to a radio show. You will hear these words. Work with a partner and check (✓) the words you already know. Use your dictionary to help you with the words you don't know.

☐ adventurer (n.)   ☐ avalanche (n.)   ☐ incredible (adj.)   ☐ set a record (v.)

B | Write each word from exercise **A** next to its definition below.

1. _____ extremely good or impressive

2. _____ be the best at something

3. _____ someone who enjoys traveling and doing exciting things

4. _____ a large amount of snow, ice, and rocks that fall down a mountain

C | **Predicting Content.** You are going to listen to a radio show about three adventure seekers. Look at the photos and put a check (✓) next to the risks you think they will encounter. After listening, check your predictions.

☐ avalanche   ☐ bears   ☐ falling   ☐ sharks

☐ extreme temperatures   ☐ falling   ☐ breathing   ☐ swimming

Listening: A Radio Show

A | **Listening for Main Ideas.** Listen to the radio show. Circle the main ideas.

track 1-14

Adventurers take risks because they seek adventure.   Lakpa and Sano are from Nepal.

You should never do an adventure by yourself.   Adventures can have dangers.

B | **Listening for Details.** Read the statements and answer choices. Then listen to the interview again and choose the correct word or phrase.

track 1-14

1. What hit Cory Richards?

   a. rocks   b. an avalanche   c. a porter

2. Why does Cory like climbing?

   a. He likes to feel that there is something bigger than him.

   b. He likes the bad weather.

   c. He likes to set records.

3. Cory believes that you _____

   a. can always conquer a mountain.

   b. are always the mountain's guest.

   c. have to be in a good mood.

4. In what order did Sano and Lakpa do their adventure?

   a. bicycle, kayak, climb, paraglide

   b. climb, bicycle, paraglide, kayak

   c. climb, paraglide, bicycle, kayak

5. Why did Sano and Lakpa do this adventure?

   a. They wanted to have fun.

   b. They wanted to set a record.

   c. They wanted to be popular.

After Listening

Discussion. Which adventure do you think is more dangerous, interesting, adventurous, and different? Put a check (✓) in the box. With a partner, compare your opinions.

	Cory's Winter Climb	Lakpa and Sano's Adventure
Dangerous		
Interesting		
Adventurous		
Different		

Grammar: The Simple Present Tense

We use the simple present tense to tell about actions that are repeated or usual. The action can be a habit, a daily event, or something that happens regularly.

Affirmative Statements (+)	Negative Statements (-)	Questions (?)
I **ski**.	They **don't paraglide**.	**Do** you **hike**?
She often **climbs** mountains.	He **doesn't take** risks.	**Does** she **scuba dive**?
We **seek** adventure.	You **don't kayak** in the winter.	**Do** they **swim**?

A | Look at the activity survey below. The checks (✓) show activities Mike does. The Xs show activities Mike doesn't do. Write five sentences about Mike using the information from his survey.

ski

surf

swim

play tennis

rock climb

hike

Example: _He doesn't ski._

1. _____

2. _____

3. _____

4. _____

5. _____

B | **Discussion.** Do you think Mike takes risks and seeks danger? Explain. Discuss your ideas with a partner.

C | Make an activity survey. Choose five activities from the list, or think of your own activities and write them in the chart. Then interview your partner and check (✓) the box according to your partner's responses.

bike	paraglide	play soccer	scuba dive	swim
hike	play golf	play tennis	ski	rock climb

Do you swim?

Yes, I swim.

Activities	Yes	No

D | **Follow-Up.** Tell the class what activities your partner does.

Marco scuba dives.

Marco doesn't hike.

track **1-15**

Pronunciation: The Third Person Singular

The *s* at the end of a verb in the third person singular of the simple present tense has three different sounds: /s/, /z/, or /iz/. Here are the rules.

/s/ sound after these final sounds: /f/, /k/, /p/, /t/

Examples: *He hikes. She paints. He surfs.*

/z/ sound after vowels and these final sounds: /l/, /m/, /n/, /r/, /th/, /v/, /d/

Examples: *She plays. He goes. She swims. He paraglides. She skis. He snowboards.*

/iz/ sound after these final sounds: /s/, /sh/, /ch/, /z/, /j/. The /iz/ sound is pronounced as a separate syllable.

Examples: *He watches. She fixes. He washes. She fishes.*

track **1-16**

A | Listen to the following verbs. Do you hear the differences in the ending sounds? Put a check (✓) under the sound you hear.

	/s/ sound	/z/ sound	/iz/ sound
climbs			
kayaks			
skis			
snowboards			
swims			
hikes			
surfs			
watches			
bikes			
bungee jumps			

track **1-17**

B | Listen to Maria's favorite activities. Put a check (✓) on the activities she does. With a partner, take turns asking and answering questions about Maria. Take note of your pronunciation with the final *s*.

Does Maria surf?

Yes, Maria surfs.

Discussing a Plan

A | **Survey.** How adventurous are you? Complete the survey. Discuss your results with a partner.

1. Your friend asks you to rock climb. Do you say yes to the invitation? **Yes** **No**

2. You are invited to a dinner with international foods. You do not know any of the foods. Do you try everything? **Yes** **No**

3. Your friend is learning how to rock climb and she wants you to join the class also. Do you take the class? **Yes** **No**

4. A group from your town is going to another country to build homes for people in need. There is no electricity at the camp and you will have to get your water from the river. Do you go? **Yes** **No**

5. You have an opportunity to take a new job, but you don't have the skills. Do you take the job? **Yes** **No**

6. You get an opportunity to live with another family in another country. Do you go? **Yes** **No**

Count how many times you answered yes. Check your adventurous score below.

5–6: You are extreme! You love to try new things and are not afraid to fail.

3–4: You are brave. You will try some new things but you are still careful.

0–2: You do not take risks. You like to do safe things.

B | **Critical Thinking.** Look at the categories below. Choose a category in which you want to be more adventurous. Look at the example plan, and then make a plan of your own.

Categories:	Travel	Food	Job	Activity

	Susan's Plan
Goal	I want to be more adventurous with food.
Ideas	• Go to different international restaurants. • Have a dinner party with an international menu. • Try a new food each week.

C | **Comparing.** Find a classmate who chose the same category as you. Compare your ideas and write any new ideas on your plan.

D | Form a group with another pair of students. Share your plan with them.

HIGHLINING
YOSEMITE FALLS

Before Viewing

A | Prior Knowledge. In Lesson **A**, you learned about people who take risks. This video is about Dean Potter, a famous highliner. Look at the photo and read the caption. With a partner, fill in the first column of the chart.

▲ Dean Potter highlining Yosemite Falls

What do you know about highlining?	What do you want to know about highlining?	What did you learn about highlining?
walk on a rope between 2 high mountains.		

B | Using a Dictionary. Match each word from the video to its definition. Use your dictionary to help you.

1. distraction (n.) __e__
2. beauty (n.) __a__
3. focus (v.) __d__
4. creativity (n.) __b__
5. lunatic (n.) __c__

a. something that is pretty and nice to look at
b. the ability to use your imagination to make, see, or do new things
c. a wild, crazy person
d. to pay close attention to something
e. something that takes your attention away from what you are doing

C | Predicting Content. Use the correct form of the words from exercise **B** to complete the information about the video.

Highlining is very difficult. Wind and moving water can be big (1) __distraction__.
Dean (2) __focus__ on his breath. Many people think Dean Potter is a
(3) __lunatic__ to highline. But Dean Potter highlines because of the
(4) __beauty__. Yosemite brings out his (5) __creativity__.

D | With a partner, fill in the second column of the chart in exercise **A**.

While Viewing

A | Checking Predictions. Watch the video and check your predictions in exercise **C** on page 32.

B | Watch the video again. Circle **T** for *true* or **F** for *false*.

1. Dean Potter lives in Yosemite Valley.   (T)   F

2. Many highliners use Amsteel, a soft cable that is 40 percent stronger than steel.   (T)   F

3. The line over Yosemite Falls is an easy line for Dean Potter.   T   (F)

4. Late spring, early summer the water is very low in the falls.   (T)   (F)

C | Using the Simple Present. Watch the video again. Circle the things that Dean does while highlining. Cross out the things that he doesn't do while highlining. Then tell a partner.

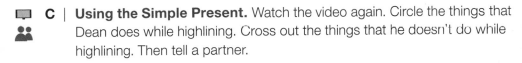

> *Dean uses Amsteel when he highlines.*

   ✓ use Amsteel   ✓ focus on his breath   ~~focus on the moving water~~

   ✓ set up his cable   ✓ walk the line   ✓ focus on the beauty

   ✓ use a safety belt   sleep on the line

D | Watch the video again. Fill in the last column of the chart in exercise **A** on page 32. Discuss what you learned with a partner.

After Viewing

A | Discussion. Form a group with two or three other students. Discuss the question.

There are many reasons people like to take risks. Some of the reasons include: to get a thrill, to see beauty, to set a record, to seek danger, or to have an adventure. Which reason do you think is the best?

B | Self-Reflection. Dean Potter says that when he highlines, he can see a new part of himself that he didn't know was there. When do you see a new part of yourself? Tell your partner about it.

> *I see a new part of myself in English class.*

> *I see a new part of myself when I go scuba diving.*

A | Listen and check (✓) the words you already know. These are words you will hear and use in Lesson **B**.

track 1-18

- ☐ act (v.)
- ☐ discoveries (n.)
- ☐ explore (v.)
- ☐ explorer (n.)
- ☐ information (n.)
- ☐ make a fortune (v.)
- ☐ needs (n.)
- ☐ satisfy (v.)

B | **Meaning from Context.** Read and listen to the article. Notice the words in **blue**.

track 1-19

Nalini Nadkami doesn't have a normal job. She is an **explorer** and her office is the rainforest. Her job can be risky. She hangs from ropes, hundreds of feet above the ground, in Costa Rica's Monteverde Cloud Forest. She learns about the plants at the top of the forest trees.

Eugenie Clark is another explorer. Her job can be risky, also. Some people call her the "Shark Lady." She learns about how sharks **act** and live. This information helps us know more about ocean animals.

There are many kinds of explorers. Some **explore** to **satisfy** our **needs** such as food and water. Some look for new **information**, or to **make a fortune**. Some search to set a record, find something new, and become famous for their **discoveries**. And, some explore to make the world a better place. These explorers risk their lives every day so that we can learn more about our planet.

C | Write each word in **blue** from exercise **B** next to its definition.

1. _____ (n.) someone who travels to new places or does new things

2. _____ (v.) to travel through an unfamiliar area to find something new

3. _____ (v.) to make someone happy by giving the person what he/she wants or needs

4. _____ (n.) what someone has to have in order to live

5. _____ (v.) to do something; to behave in a certain way

6. _____ (n.) things that have never been found before

7. _____ (v.) to get a large amount of money by doing something

8. _____ (n.) facts or details that tell you something about a person, place, thing, or event

A | Read the sentences. Circle the correct word.

1. People (explore / satisfy) to find new ideas.

2. Some people explore to (make a fortune / satisfy) from what they find.

3. Many animals (act / explore) like humans. They do the same things.

4. Eugenie Clark has made many (information / discoveries) that help make our world a better place.

5. The (needs / discoveries) of animals are similar to humans.

6. Having (information / explorers) about animals helps humans understand our world.

7. Humans often explored to (make a fortune / satisfy) their needs.

8. (Explorers / Discoveries) can have risky jobs.

B | **Discussion.** With a partner, discuss the questions below.

1. What are your daily **needs**?

2. What are some famous **discoveries**? Who discovered them?

3. Who has **made a fortune**? How did he/she make the fortune?

C | **Ranking Information.** What is the best reason to explore? Rank the reasons for exploring in order of importance (1 = most important; 5 = least important). Then compare your ideas with your partner.

Rank	Reasons to explore
	to be famous
	to make a fortune
	to get information
	to satisfy needs
	to make the world better

What is your number one reason to explore?

I think "to make the world better" is number one.

Before Listening

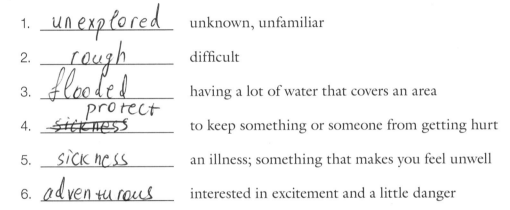

A | **Using a Dictionary.** You will hear these words in the conversation that follows. Work with a partner and check (✓) the words you already know. Use your dictionary to help you with the words you don't know.

☐ adventurous (adj.)   ☐ protect (v.)   ☐ sickness (n.)

☐ flooded (adj.)   ☐ rough (adj.)   ☐ unexplored (adj.)

Critical Thinking Focus

Making Predictions

Before you listen, predict what you will hear. Making predictions about what the speakers will say helps you focus on the topic before you listen.

B | Write each word from exercise **A** next to its definition below.

1. _un explored_   unknown, unfamiliar

2. _rough_   difficult

3. _flooded_   having a lot of water that covers an area

4. _sickness_ ~~protect~~   to keep something or someone from getting hurt

5. _sickness_   an illness; something that makes you feel unwell

6. _adventurous_   interested in excitement and a little danger

C | **Predicting Content.** You are going to listen to a conversation about Emma Stokes, an explorer. Before listening, predict what you will hear and then compare your ideas with a partner.

1. What are the risks of Emma's job? Check (✓) the risks.

☑ sickness   ☑ elephants

☐ sharks   ☑ flooded areas

2. Why do you think Emma explores? Check (✓) the reasons.

☐ to become famous

☑ to learn information

☑ to protect animals

☐ to make a fortune

▲ National Geographic explorer Emma Stokes

Listening: A Conversation

Track 1-20

A | Listening for the Main Idea. Listen to the conversation. Circle the main idea.

1. Emma Stokes found 125,000 lowland gorillas in Congo.

2. Rebecca wants to be an explorer, like Emma Stokes.

3. The work of Emma Stokes.

Track 1-20

B | Listening for Details. Listen to the conversation again. Circle the details you hear.

She camped on an elephant nest.	They slept in beds hung from trees.
She is protecting tigers now.	She has been a conservationist for many years.
She is helping elephants.	
She discovered 125,000 gorillas.	Companies and sickness are dangerous to the gorillas.
The area was flooded.	

Track 1-20

C | Checking Predictions. Look back at the predictions you made in exercise **C** on page 36. Then listen again. Which of your predictions were correct?

After Listening

| Critical Thinking. Think of an area of the world that you would like to explore. Complete the sentences below. Form a group with two or three other students. Share your ideas.

> I want to explore the jungles of Africa. I want to explore them because I want to see the animals. I want to go with my friend, Luis. I want to go next year.

Where: I want to explore

forreign countries.

Why: I want to explore it/them because

This is interesting

Who: I want to go with

_____

When: I want to go

_____

Grammar: The Simple Present with *Wh-* Questions

We use *what, where, when, why,* and *how* to find out more information.

Sample *Wh-* Questions	Sample Responses
What do you **do** on the weekends?	*I hike.*
Where does he **swim**?	*He swims in the lake.*
When do we **go** to the mountains?	*We go on Saturday.*
Why do they **explore**?	*They want to learn more about animals.*
How does she **protect** the gorillas?	*She protects their home.*

Write *Wh-* questions using the simple present tense.

1. do / you / when / hike ?
   <u>When do you hike?</u>

2. he / where / swim / does ?
   _____

3. rock climb / they / how / do ?
   _____

4. activity / do / what / you / do ?
   _____

5. she / paraglide / does / why ?
   _____

6. weekend / do / they / what / do / on / the ?
   _____

7. does / why / take / risks / she ?
   _____

8. bike / where / he / does ?
   _____

Language Function: Showing Interest

It is important to show interest in a conversation. Here are some phrases you can use to show that you are interested in what the other person is saying.

That's interesting.   *Really? Why?*   *Great!*   *Tell me more.*

A | Check (✓) the activities you do.

Activities

- ☐ Swim
- ☐ Play tennis
- ☐ Hike
- ☐ Bike
- ☐ Rock climb
- ☐ Take risks
- ☐ Ski
- ☐ Surf

B | With a partner, ask each other questions about the activities you do. Use a phrase from the Language Function box to show that you are interested before asking another question. Use the model below.

Do you ski?

Yes, I do.

Really? Why do you ski?

It is fun.

Student to Student

Making Eye Contact

It is polite to look at the person you are listening to. If you look down or away, they may think that you are not interested in the conversation.

2

In this section, you will work with a group to plan a presentation about an adventure trip.

A | Choose. Form a group with two or three other students. Look at the ideas for adventure trips below. Circle an adventure trip you want to go on, or think of your own idea.

rock climb	hike	kayak a river
paraglide	raft	scuba dive
mountain bike	cliff jump	

B | Planning Your Trip. Use the model below to plan your adventure trip.

What can you do?	We can scuba dive.
Where can you go?	We can go to Australia.
When can you go?	We can go next summer.
How can you do it?	We can learn to dive this summer. We can get a guide in Australia.

C | Planning a Presentation. Decide which member of your group will present each part of your plan. Practice your presentation together.

D | Presentation. Present your ideas to the class.

Presentation Skills: Asking for Questions

Asking for questions is a way to end a presentation. Here are some phrases you can use to ask for questions from the audience.

Are there any questions?

Do you have any questions?

We can take your questions now.

Enjoy the Ride!

ACADEMIC PATHWAYS
Lesson A: Listening to an Interview
        Choosing the Best Idea
Lesson B: Listening to a Conversation
        Giving a Group Presentation

Exploring the Theme:
Enjoy the Ride!

Look at the photos and read the captions and the information. Then discuss the questions.

1. Which vehicles in the photos do you know? Do you ride on any of them?

2. What public transportation do you have in your city? Do you use it?

3. Which country has the most people using public transportation? Which country has the least?

CHINA
INDIA
RUSSIA
SOUTH KOREA
MEXICO
BRAZIL
JAPAN
UNITED KINGDOM
CANADA
USA

Riding in a tuk-tuk in India

Riding on a sampan in China

Percentage of People Using **Public Transportation**

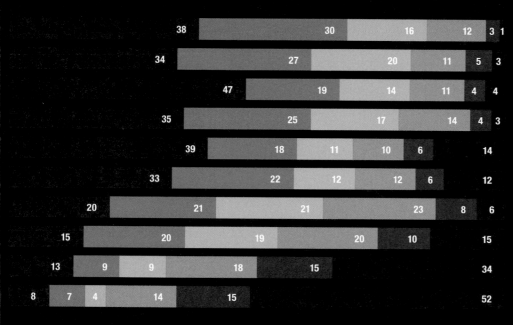

38	30	16	12	3	1	
34	27	20	11	5	3	
47	19	14	11	4	4	
35	25	17	14	4	3	
39	18	11	10	6	14	
33	22	12	12	6	12	
20	21	21	23	8	6	
15	20	19	20	10	15	
13	9	9	18	15	34	
8	7	4	14	15	52	

Most days
Once a week
Once a month
A few times a year
Once a year or less
Never

Source: Greendex 2010, NGS and GlobeScan

Note: 1–3% of people in some countries responded "don't know." This data is not included in the chart.

Riding on a moped in Brazil

A | Using a Dictionary. Listen and check (✓) the words you already know. Use a dictionary to help you with any new words. These are words you will hear and use in Lesson **A**.

track **1-21**

☐ commute (v.) ☐ crowded (adj.) ☐ pedestrian (n.) ☐ share (v.)
☐ convenient (adj.) ☐ passenger (n.) ☐ safe (adj.) ☐ vehicle (n.)

B | Meaning from Context. Read and listen to the people. Notice the words in **blue**. Then write each word from exercise **A** next to its definition below.

track **1-22**

How do you **commute**? There are many ways to travel. A bus, a car, and a train are usual ways to move from one place to another. There are many other **vehicles**, too. Read how these people get around in their countries.

I am Bora and I am from Cambodia. In my village we make our own trains. We call them Norries. A Norry has a wooden frame, a bamboo floor, and a small engine. The Norry goes on a train track. The **passengers** jump off when a real train comes!

I am Ana and I am from Colombia. I commute by a cable car in the sky. My city has many hills. The cable car helps move the people throughout the city.

I am Ling and I am from China. I bicycle to work. Cars, bikes, and **pedestrians share** the road. It is very **crowded** but it is **convenient** and **safe**.

1. _vehicle_   something that takes people or things from one place to another

2. _safe_   not dangerous or in danger

3. _pedestrian_   a person who walks

4. _passenger_   a person who is traveling in a car, plane, or boat but is not driving it

5. _commute_   to travel regularly in order to get to work, school, etc.

6. _share_   to use something that other people use at the same time

7. _convenient_   easy to use

8. _crowded_   too full of people or things

A | Read the conversation. Fill in each blank with the correct form of a word from exercise **A** on page 44.

A: How do you (1) __commute__ to work every day?

B: I take the bus. It is very (2) __crowded__ in the morning. There are a lot of people.

A: Where is the bus stop?

B: There is a bus stop in front of my apartment.

A: That's very (3) __convenient__!

B: Yes, I am lucky. How about you? How do you get to work?

A: I don't have a (4) __vehicle__ and there isn't a bus stop near me. So, I walk.

B: Do you feel (5) __safe__ at night?

A: There are a lot of other (6) __pedestrians__ on the sidewalks. Many people walk to work.

B: There are also a lot of bicycles on the road.

A: Yes, there are. I hope the vehicles (7) __share__ the road with them.

B: I agree. I don't think it is safe to ride a bike in this city. I am happy to be a (8) __passenger__ and let someone else drive me!

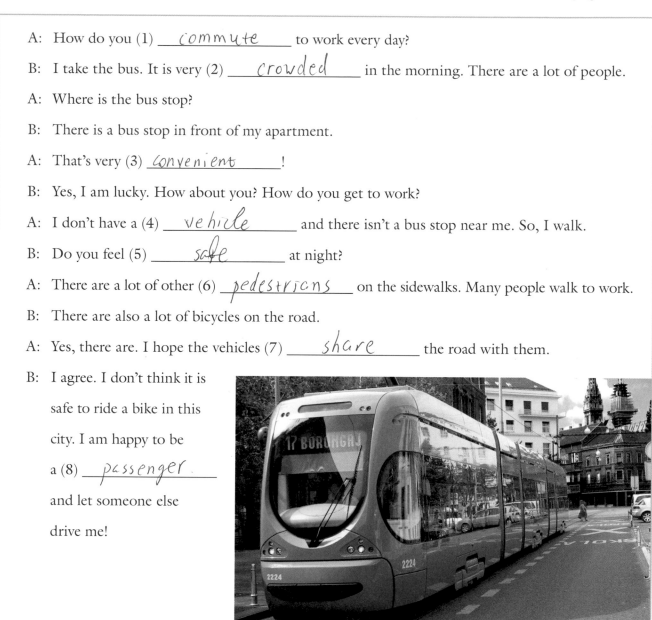

B | Work with a partner. Compare your answers from exercise **A**. Then practice the conversation.

C | **Discussion.** With your partner, discuss the questions below.

1. How do you commute to work or school? How is the trip? Safe? Convenient? Crowded?

2. Do you like to be the driver or a passenger? Explain.

> I commute by train. It is crowded, but it is very convenient.

> I like to be a passenger. I don't like to drive.

D | **Ranking Information.** Which vehicle do you think is safe? Rank the vehicles on a scale of 1 through 5 in order of safety (1 = very safe; 5 = not safe). Discuss with a group.

_____ tuk-tuk _____ bus _____ car _____ airplane _____ bicycle

track 1-23

Pronunciation: *There is* and *There are*

When people speak English quickly, they don't always pronounce every word fully. In fast speech, the phrases *there is* and *there are* are often blended together.

There is becomes *There's* and is pronounced: [therez]

There are is pronounced: [therere]

Listen to the sentences. Pay attention to the blended sounds.

Careful Speech	**Fast Speech**
There's a car.	***Thereza*** car.
There's an airplane.	***Therezan*** airplane.
There are many vehicles.	***Therere*** many vehicles.
There are many pedestrians.	***Therere*** many pedestrians.

 With a partner, practice saying the sentences below. Blend the sounds together.

1. There is a bus.
2. There are many passengers.
3. There is a bicycle.

4. There are many tuk-tuks.
5. There is a pedestrian.
6. There are many boats.

Before Listening

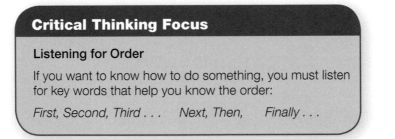

Critical Thinking Focus

Listening for Order

If you want to know how to do something, you must listen for key words that help you know the order:

First, Second, Third . . .   Next, Then,   Finally . . .

Read and listen to these directions. Fill in the blanks with the words that help the listener know the order.
track 1-24

The mountain music festival is a lot of fun! There are so many interesting bands and people. The best way to get there is to go by car. But, you can get to the music festival by other modes of transportation, too. (1) _____, take the train to Moorestown. The train takes about three hours. (2) _____, get on the #9 bus to Hill Ridge City. The bus takes about 45 minutes. (3) _____, find a taxi to take you to the top of the mountain. The taxi ride is only about 20 minutes. (4) _____, walk a half a mile to the festival.

Listening: An Interview

A | Listening for Main Ideas. Read the questions and answer choices. Then listen to the interview and choose the correct answers.

1. What does Maria write about in her article *Trains and Tuk-Tuks*?
   a. Traveling around the world.
   b. Types of vehicles you use when traveling around the world.
   c. How to drive various vehicles around the world.

2. What is the interview about?
   a. Maria McNeal's life.
   b. How to drive a tuk-tuk and trek in Nepal.
   c. The interesting modes of transportation that Maria uses.

B | Listening for Details. Read the statements and listen again. Then circle **T** for *true* or **F** for *false*.

1. People use dog sleds in Canada and Finland.	**T**	**F**
2. Not many people use tuk-tuks in Asia.	**T**	**F**
3. Some tuk-tuks have motors.	**T**	**F**
4. Maria rides on top of the bus because it is not safe to ride in the bus.	**T**	**F**
5. To hike Annapurna, first walk to the bus station. Second, get on a train, and then take a tuk-tuk to the base of the mountain.	**T**	**F**

After Listening

A | Critical Thinking. Think of a place in your country. How do you get there? Write the steps and the types of transportation you use to get there.

B | Explaining. Tell your partner the place you wrote about in exercise **A**. Explain how to get there.

EXPLORING SPOKEN ENGLISH

Grammar: *There is, There are, There was, There were*

There is and *There are* indicate that something exists or is in a certain location. *There was* and *There were* indicate that something existed or was in a certain location in the past.

There is	There are	There was	There were
There is a bus stop by my house.	**There are** many tuk-tuks in India.	**There was** a dog in front of my car yesterday.	**There were** many passengers on the bus yesterday.
There's a ferry to the island.	**There are** many dog-sled races in Alaska.	**There was** a train crash in my town last month.	**There were** many pedestrians on the street this morning.

A | Circle the best phrase for the sentence. Then say your sentences to a partner. Some sentences have more than one correct answer.

1. (**There is** /(**There are**)/ **There was** / **There were**) many pedestrians on the street right now.

2. (**There is** / **There are** / **There was** / **There were**) a ferry to the island on Saturdays.

3. (**There is** / **There are** / **There was** / **There were**) a lot of bicycles on the bike path yesterday.

4. (**There is** / **There are** / **There was** / **There were**) a chicken on the bus last week.

5. (**There is** / **There are** / **There was** / **There were**) a lot of dogs on that sled team.

6. (**There is** / **There are** / **There was** / **There were**) a truck in front of my car. I can't move.

B | Complete each sentence. Use *there is, there are, there was,* or *there were* and your own ideas about your city or country. Then practice your sentences with your partner.

In my country _____.

In my country, _____ in the past.

In my city, _____.

In my city _____ in the past.

▲ In India, cyclists, mopeds, and elephants share the road.

C | Look at the photo. Write three sentences using *There is* and *There are*.

1. _____.

2. _____.

3. _____.

D | Read your sentences to a partner. See if your partner can find the things in the picture.

Language Function: Asking Questions to Encourage Communication

If someone asks you a question, it is polite to ask the same question back. This shows your interest in the person you are talking to. Here are some questions you can use to encourage communication.

How about you?   *What about you?*   *What do you think?*

A: *Do you take the bus to school?*
B: *No, I don't. I drive to school.* **How about you?**
A: *I drive, too.*

A: *I like to drive.* **What about you?**
B: *I like to be the passenger.*

A | Answer each question below with your own information. Then choose a question from the Language Function box on page 49 to encourage communication.

1. A: How do you get to school?

   B: _____ . _____ ?

2. A: Do you ride a bike?

   B: _____ . _____ ?

3. A: Do you think motorcycles are safe?

   B: _____ . _____ ?

B | Practice the conversations in exercise **A** with a partner. Take turns being A and B.

Example:

A: How do you get to school?

B: I ride my moped to school. What about you?

A: I take the bus.

C | **Critical Thinking.** Form a group with two or three other students. Discuss the questions. Ask questions to encourage everyone to communicate.

1. Are there speed limits in your country? Do you think it is good to have speed limits?

2. Do you always wear a seat belt in a car? Do you think school buses need seat belts?

3. Is the public transportation (bus, train, subway, etc.) good in your city? Is it safe?

4. Do you think public transportation is important? Explain.

Choosing the Best Idea

A | Read about the problem with pollution in our cities. Then read the four ideas on how to help with this problem.

There are many vehicles in cities. Vehicles make pollution. Pollution is dirty air and it is bad for living things. Read about how some cities encourage the use of public transportation to decrease pollution.

Idea 1 Free Public Transportation ▶

In **Hasselt, Belgium**, you can ride the bus free! The city government hopes people will stop driving their cars to work and start using the free public transportation.

Idea 2 Decrease Parking ▶

In **San Francisco**, there are many vehicles, but there are not a lot of parking spaces. The city government is decreasing the parking areas. They hope that this will get more people to use public transportation.

Idea 3 Carpool Lanes ▶

Carpooling is when people commute to work in the same car. This decreases the number of vehicles on the road. Cities like **Washington, D.C.**, have special carpool lanes. The carpool cars get to work faster.

Idea 4 Trade in Your Car ▶

In **Murcia, Spain**, you can give your vehicle to the city and ride the new public transportation free!

B | **Critical Thinking.** With a partner, discuss the ideas above. Which do you think is the best?

C | **Collaboration.** How can you decrease pollution in your city? How can you get people to use public transportation? With your partner, think of your own ideas.

D | **Presentation.** Form a group with two or three other pairs. Share your plan with them.

Indian Railways

Before Viewing

A | Prior Knowledge. In Lesson **A** you learned about how people travel around in different countries. This video is about trains in India. With a partner, discuss the questions.

1. What are trains like around the world?
2. Why do people take trains?
3. What do people do on trains?
4. What steps do you take to ride a train in your city?

B | Using a Dictionary. Match each word from the video to its definition. Use your dictionary to help you.

1. rural (adj.) _____	a. very small, tiny
2. stressful (adj.) _____	b. train system
3. miniature (adj.) _____	c. in the country, not the city
4. railways (n.) _____	d. workers
5. rush hour (n.) _____	e. great, exciting
6. impressive (adj.) _____	f. a very busy and crowded time when most people commute
7. staff (n.) _____	g. hard, tiring

C | Predicting Content. Use the words from exercise **B** to complete the information about the video.

Mumbai, India

The trains in India are very busy. It is always (1) _____ in the Mumbai train station. Because it is so crowded, train travel can be (2) _____.

The British built the (3) _____ in the 1800s. Now they go all over India. Some trains have (4) _____ names like the Himalayan Queen. Many people live in cities, but even people in (5) _____ areas travel on trains. Many people work for the railways. There are 1.5 million (6) _____. All kinds of people ride on trains. It is like a (7) _____ India.

While Viewing

A | Watch the video. Check your predictions from exercise **C** on page 52.

B | In Lesson **A**, you listened for words to know order, such as *first*, *next*, and *finally*. You can also know the order of events through time expressions. Read the statements below. Watch the video again. Write the time expression from the box on the line.

Now	1853	19th century	1929

1. The British build the railway system in India. _____

2. The first steam engine runs in India. _____

3. The train called the Grand Trunk Express begins to travel on the tracks. _____

4. Passengers travel 38,000 miles of track across India. _____

C | Watch the video again. Circle the correct word to complete the sentences.

1. Most people in India commute by (**train** / **car**).

2. Indian trains and stations are (**quiet** / **crowded**).

3. There are more than 4 billion (**trips** / **passengers**) each year on the Indian railways.

4. There are sometimes performance artists in the (**stations** / **trains**).

After Viewing

A | **Discussion.** Form a group with two or three other students. Discuss the questions.

1. Why are trains so popular in India?

2. What are some good and bad things about trains?

3. In the video you heard "But the railway is more than just a way to travel. It is like a miniature India." What does this mean? Are there any places like that in your country?

B | **Critical Thinking.** In this section, you learned about an important form of transportation in India. In Lesson **B** of this unit, you will learn about some new and unusual forms of transportation in other countries. With your group, discuss this question.

Why do we develop different forms of transportation? Consider these things:

technology	where people live	money	the environment

A | **Using a Dictionary.** Listen and check (✓) the words you already know. Use a dictionary to help you with any new words. These are words you will hear and use in Lesson **B**.

track 1-26

- ☐ destination (n.)
- ☐ lie down (v.)
- ☐ miles/kilometers per hour (n.)
- ☐ old-fashioned (adj.)
- ☐ get around (v.)
- ☐ machine (n.)
- ☐ modern (adj.)
- ☐ take it easy (v.)

B | **Meaning from Context.** Read and listen to the article. Notice the words in **blue**.

track 1-27

A bus, a car, a train? How old-fashioned! We want something new!
Read about some modern ways to get around town.

Personal Jet Pack: This machine takes you up above the vehicles below. You can fly! There are not many of these in the world, but maybe in the future we will all fly!

Self-Driving Car: Sleep, read, lie down while driving? You can in this self-driving car. A computer drives the car and you take it easy in the back seat.

Maglev Train: This is a train that doesn't touch the tracks. It gets you to your destination in record time. There is a Maglev Train in Shanghai, China. It takes passengers from Shanghai airport to downtown. It travels at 431 kilometers per hour.

C | Match each word with its definition.

1. get around
2. machine
3. destination
4. miles/kilometers per hour
5. lie down
6. take it easy
7. modern
8. old-fashioned

a. to relax
b. old; belonging to an earlier time
c. to move or travel to different places
d. new; current or recent time
e. your speed; how far you can go in an hour
f. the place you are going to
g. to put your body flat on the floor, bed, etc.
h. a piece of equipment that helps you do something

USING VOCABULARY

A | Read the sentences. Circle the correct word.

1. The jet pack is very (old-fashioned / **modern**). It is the vehicle of the future.

2. I use my bike to (take it easy / **get around**). How about you?

3. I like to be a passenger in the car because I like to (**lie down** / get around). Sometimes I even sleep in the car.

4. The Maglev Train can get you to your (machine / **destination**) very quickly.

5. I don't like the new transportation ideas. I prefer the (**old-fashioned** / modern) way of walking.

6. The jet pack is a (kilometers per hour / **machine**) that takes you up in the air.

7. I commute by train so I can (get around / **take it easy**). I read, play games, and sometimes even sleep!

8. The Maglev Train travels at 268 (**miles per hour** / destination). It is really fast!

B | **Discussion.** With a partner, discuss the questions below.

1. How do you take it easy?

2. What should the speed limit (miles/kilometers per hour) be on city streets? Neighborhood streets? Highways? Explain.

3. What machines do you use every day?

4. What is a popular destination in your country? How do you get there?

C | **Critical Thinking.** What are the pros and cons of **modern** vehicles? With a partner, complete the chart. Then, discuss with a group of three or four of your classmates.

Modern Vehicles	
Pros (+)	Cons (-)

Pro: A modern vehicle is fast.

Con: A modern vehicle is a lot of money.

Before Listening

👥 **A** | **Using a Dictionary.** You will hear these words in a conversation. Work with a partner and check (✓) the words you already know. Use a dictionary to help you with any new words.

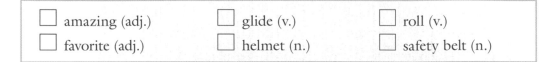

☐ amazing (adj.)　　☐ glide (v.)　　☐ roll (v.)

☐ favorite (adj.)　　☐ helmet (n.)　　☐ safety belt (n.)

B | Write each word from exercise **A** next to its definition below.

1. _____ to move smoothly and quietly

2. _____ something you attach around yourself for protection

3. _____ a hard hat that covers and protects your head

4. _____ liked more than others

5. _____ surprising in a good way

6. _____ to move by turning over and over or from side to side

👥 **C** | **Prior Knowledge.** With a partner, discuss each photo. Do you know what they are? Do you know which country they are from?*

Listening: A Conversation

🎧 track 1-28 **A** | **Listening for the Main Idea.** Listen to the conversation. Circle the main topic.

1. Zorbs in New Zealand and zip lines in Costa Rica

2. Jen's trip around the world

3. Jen's favorite parts of her trip

*ANSWERS: a Zorb in New Zealand; a zip line in Costa Rica

B | Listening for Details. Listen to the conversation again. Categorize the words. Which words are for a Zorb? Which words are for a zip line?

glide	cable	ball	roll
top of the trees	land or water	safety belt	jump off
Costa Rica	New Zealand	get inside	climb up

Zorb	Zip Line
1.	1.
2.	2.
3.	3.
4.	4.
5.	5.
	6.
	7.

After Listening

A | Discussion. Form a group with two or three other students. Discuss the questions.

1. Which activity (Zorb or zip line) is more interesting to you?

2. Tell your group about an unusual vehicle people ride on or in.

People ride skateboards. I ride one to class.

B | Critical Thinking. Look at the graph with your group. What can you say about zip lines and tourism? What are the pros and cons of tourists?

Visitors per year	2008	2009	2010	2011	2012
4,000					
3,000					
2,000					
1,000					

Tree Top, a company in the rain forest of Costa Rica, built a zip line in 2010.

EXPLORING SPOKEN ENGLISH

Grammar: *Like to, Want to, Need to*

When we use *like*, *want*, and *need* with another verb, the second verb is in the infinitive form.

Affirmative	Negative	Question
I **like to walk.** He **wants to try** a zip line. They **need to wear** a helmet.	I **don't like to walk.** He **doesn't want to try** a zip line. They **don't need to wear** a helmet.	Do you **like to walk?** Does he **want to try** a zip line? Do they **need to wear** a helmet?

A | Write the words in the correct order.

1. she / to / wants / bicycle / ride / her
   She wants to ride her bicycle.

2. to / need / they / safety belt / a / wear
   They need to wear a safety belt.

3. he / does / like / take / bus / to / the / ?
   He like Does he like to take the bus?

4. want / I / ride / Zorb / in / to / a / don't
   I don't want to ride in a Zorb.

5. I / need / do / to / helmet / wear / a / ?
   Do I need to d wear a helmet?

6. doesn't / to / like / she / fly
   She doesn't like to fly.

7. ride / she / to / wants / a / jet pack / in
   She wants to ride in a jet pack.

8. to / walk / need / they / school / to
   They need to walk to school.

B | **Critical Thinking.** Look at the photos for how to be safe on a zip line. What do you need to do first, second, third, and fourth? Write the steps on page 59. Use *need to*.

▲ long-sleeved shirt, long pants   ▲ sports shoes   ▲ helmet

safety belt and harness ▶

Example: *First, you need to wear a long-sleeved shirt and long pants.*

1. _____

2. _____

3. _____

Language Function: Encouraging

It is nice to encourage your classmates and friends to try something new. Here are some phrases you can use to encourage people.

You can do it!   *Don't worry!*   *It is fun!*   *Try your best!*

Examples:

1. A: *I don't want to do the zip line.*
    B: **Don't worry!** *It's safe!*

2. A: *I don't want to ride a bike. I am afraid.*
    B: **You can do it!**

Student to Student

Saying Thanks

It is polite to say thank you when someone helps you or encourages you.

A | With a partner, practice the sample conversations in the Language Function box above. Then create a conversation of your own.

A: _____.

B: _____.

B | Work with a partner. Think of a vehicle. What are the things you need to do to be safe in that vehicle? Make a list. Use *need to*.

Safety List
Vehicle: Motorcyele.
Things you need to do:
1. ~~First, you~~ We need to wear leather jacket. (long sleeved)
2. ~~Second,~~ we need to wear comfortofle flat sheas.
3. ~~Third,~~ We need to wear helmet.
4. We need to be careful.

C | Read your safety list to the class. After the pairs read their lists, think of a question for each pair.

Do I need to wear a helmet?

In this section, you will give a presentation about a modern vehicle. You will work with a group to create a vehicle and then present your plan to the class.

A | **Brainstorming.** Form a group with three or four other students. Brainstorm some ideas for a modern vehicle.

B | **Organizing Details.** Choose one of your ideas. Begin to think of the details of your vehicle. Look at the sample chart. Complete your own chart for your vehicle.

Vehicle Name	Zorb
Type of vehicle (land, water, air)	Land, water
Description of vehicle (What does it look like? How does it go?)	A round, plastic ball. First, you get into the ball. Then, you run and the Zorb moves.
How many people can go in or on it?	1–2 people
Safety issues (What do you need to do to be safe?)	Wear a helmet.

Vehicle Name	
Type of vehicle (land, water, air)	
Description of vehicle (What does it look like? How does it go?)	
How many people can go in or on it?	
Safety issues (What do you need to do to be safe?)	

C | **Planning a Presentation.** Decide which member of your group will present each part of your plan from exercise **B**. Practice your presentation together.

D | **Presentation.** Present your ideas to the class.

Presentation Skills: Introducing Your Group

Introducing your group and your topic before you begin your presentation is important. It shows the audience that you are ready to begin and gives them an idea of what you will talk about.

Hello. We are Maria, Jen, Tom, and Kathy.

We want to tell you about . . .

Unusual Destinations

ACADEMIC PATHWAYS
Lesson A: Listening to a Presentation
           Choosing the Best Vacation
Lesson B: Listening to a Group Conversation
           Giving an Individual Presentation

Think and Discuss

1. Do you know what these lights are in the sky?
2. Where can you see these lights?
3. What do you think the unit is about?

▲ Northern lights in the night sky over Norway

Exploring the Theme: Unusual Destinations

Look at the photos and read the captions and the information. Then discuss the questions.

1. Where do you like to travel?

2. What differences do you see between the photos? How are they alike and how are they different?

3. Look at the two photos. Which place do you want to go to?

Explore the Unusual

Are you bored with the same vacation spot? Our world has so many beautiful places. Some of them are natural like this cave in the Bahamas and some of them are manmade like this cave in Turkey. Many people go to the same place every year. This year, be adventurous and plan your next vacation at an unusual destination. Then, spend the rest of your life enjoying the natural and manmade wonders across our world. So many places and so little time!

▲ A manmade cave in Turkey.

▲ A diver explores an underwater cave in the Bahamas.

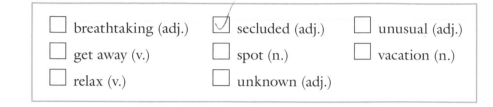

A | **Using a Dictionary.** Listen and check (✓) the words you already know. Use a dictionary to help you with any new words. These are words you will hear and use in Lesson **A**.

track 1-29

☐ breathtaking (adj.)	✓ secluded (adj.)	☐ unusual (adj.)
☐ get away (v.)	☐ spot (n.)	☐ vacation (n.)
☐ relax (v.)	☐ unknown (adj.)	

B | **Meaning from Context.** Read about and listen to these two people. Notice the words in **blue**. Then write each word in blue next to its definition below.

track 1-30

Where do you like to go on vacation? Do you like to go to a popular place or an unusual spot? Listen to these two people talk about their favorite destinations.

My favorite spot is Ochheuteal Beach, Cambodia. Not many people know about this beach. It is quiet and I can relax there. There are parts of the beach that are completely secluded. I don't like to go to tourist destinations, so this beach is perfect for me.

I like to travel to unknown places. My favorite place to get away is Spencer Glacier in Alaska. In this photo we are very close to the glaciers. They are breathtaking!

1. ~~secluded~~ *relax* very beautiful

2. breathtaking to be calm and not worried

3. unusual different

4. ~~get away~~ *secluded* very private and quiet

5. vacation *get away* to go on a trip

6. ~~vacation~~ *vacation, relax* a time when you don't go to work or to school

7. unknown not many people know about it; not famous

8. spot a place

A | Read the telephone conversation below. Fill in each blank with the correct form of a word from exercise **A** on page 64.

A: Hello?

B: Hi John. Where are you? You weren't in class yesterday.

A: Oh, I'm on (1) _____vacation_____ right now.

B: Great! Is it a place I know or is it an (2) _____unknown_____ place?

A: I like to go to unusual (3) _____spot_____.
It's a (4) _____secluded_____ beach. In my opinion, the fewer people, the better!

B: That sounds nice.

A: Yes, I am sitting on the beach right now. The view of the ocean is (5) _____breathtaking_____.
It is so beautiful!

B: What a great way to (6) _____get away_____ from school and work!

A: Yes, I can really (7) _____relax_____. I read and rest every day. In fact, I was asleep before your call!

B: Oh, I'm so sorry! Have a great vacation.

A: Thanks. See you next week.

B | Work with a partner. Compare your answers from exercise **A**. Then practice the conversation.

C | **Discussion.** With your partner, discuss the questions below.

1. Where do you like to get away? Do you like to go to known or unknown places? Explain.

2. Tell about a breathtaking spot in your country. Is it an unusual or a popular vacation spot?

3. In the conversation in exercise **A** above, John says, "In my opinion, the fewer people, the better!" Do you agree? Explain.

4. Do you like to go to secluded spots? Or do you prefer popular spots? Why?

> I like to go to the mountains to get away.

> I don't agree with John. I like to be with people.

DEVELOPING LISTENING SKILLS

Before Listening

Using Visuals to Activate Prior Knowledge

Often a speaker uses visuals such as maps, photos, and graphs with a lecture or talk. Before listening, look at the visuals. This information can help you understand what the lecture is going to be about

A | Understanding Visuals. You are going to listen to Tom Jenkins talk about his vacation in Southeast Asia. Look at the map and the photos and read the statements below. Circle **T** for *true* or **F** for *false*.

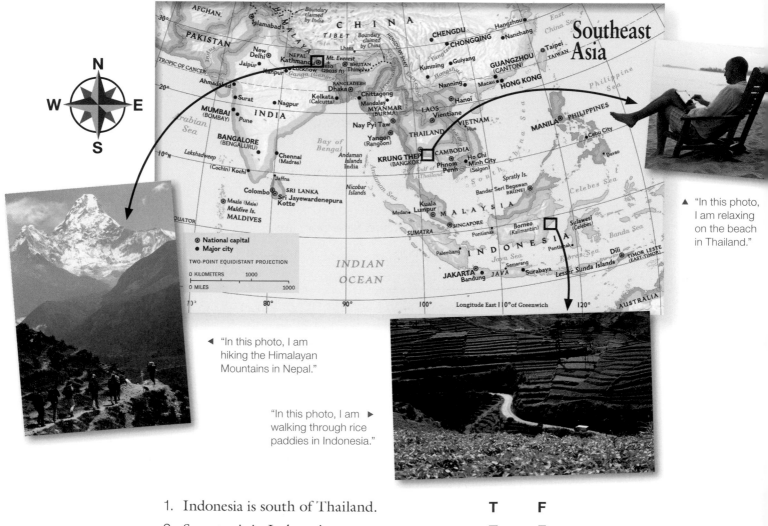

▲ "In this photo, I am relaxing on the beach in Thailand."

◄ "In this photo, I am hiking the Himalayan Mountains in Nepal."

"In this photo, I am ► walking through rice paddies in Indonesia."

1. Indonesia is south of Thailand.	**T**	**F**
2. Sumatra is in Indonesia.	**T**	**F**
3. Thailand is an island.	**T**	**F**
4. Nepal is south of China.	**T**	**F**
5. Indonesia has rice paddies.	**T**	**F**
6. The Himalayan Mountains are in Nepal.	**T**	**F**

B | Prior Knowledge. Work with a partner. What do you know about these countries? Look at the photos. Describe what you see.

Listening: A Presentation

A | Listening for Main Ideas. Read the questions and answer choices. Then listen and choose the correct answers.

track 1-31

1. Why is Tom Jenkins a speaker at this convention?

   a. He is selling his new book.

   b. He is speaking on the same topic as the convention's theme.

   c. He is a famous traveler.

2. What kind of traveler is Tom Jenkins?

   a. He likes to be in cities.

   b. He likes to go to popular spots.

   c. He likes to go to secluded places.

B | Listening for Details. Listen again. Choose the correct word or phrase to complete each sentence.

track 1-31

1. The speaker writes _____ about his adventures.

   a. news stories   b. books   c. magazine articles

2. The speaker says that Hong Kong, Bangkok, and Singapore are _____.

   a. popular spots   b. unknown spots   c. secluded spots

3. In Indonesia the speaker is _____.

   a. walking on the beach   b. walking through the city   c. walking through a rice paddy

4. The speaker says that most travelers don't leave the _____.

   a. cities   b. hotel room   c. countryside

After Listening

Critical Thinking. Form a group with two or three other students. Discuss the questions below.

1. Which book do you think Tom Jenkins wrote? Explain.

   Tourist Hot Spots   *The Unknown Road*   *Traveling with a Tour Group*

2. Robert Frost wrote a poem, "The Road Not Taken." Read the last part of the poem below. What do you think it means? Do you agree?

   I took the one less traveled by,

   And that has made all the difference.

   > I think it means that unknown destinations are the best.

Grammar: The Present Continuous

We use the present continuous to talk about things that are happening right now.

am / is / are + verb + -ing

I am (I'm)
You are (You're)
He / She / It is (He's, She's, It's)
We / They are (We're, They're)
} listening.

I **am hiking** up the mountain.
Shiva **is taking** a vacation.
The people **are relaxing** on the beach.
They**'re getting away** this weekend.

A | Maria is on a vacation with her friends. She is putting her photos on her blog. Look at her photos. Read her first caption and then finish writing a caption for each photo.

It's now 8:00 A.M. and

I am eating breakfast on my balcony .

It's now 11:00 A.M. and

_____ .

It's now 2:00 P.M. and

_____ .

It's now 4:00 P.M. and

_____ .

B | Complete the conversation with the present continuous form of the verbs in parentheses. Then practice the conversation with a partner.

A: Hi. What are you doing?

B: I (1) _____ (look) at my photos from Egypt.

A: What?

B: Remember? My vacation to Egypt last month?

A: Oh, that's right. Can I see?

B: Sure. Take a seat.

A: What are you doing in this photo?

B: Oh, I (2) _____ (ride) on a camel.

A: Did you say you (3) _____ (ride) a camel?

B: Yes!

A: Was it bumpy?

B: Very! In this photo, my friends and I (4) _____ (walk) on the beach.

A: Breathtaking view! What about this photo?

B: My friend (5) _____ (drive) a motorcycle through Cairo.

A: Oh my. A bit dangerous, huh?

B: Yes, at times. Oh, in this photo my friends and I (6) _____ (hike) up the pyramids.

A: A long way up!

B: Yes, it was. Here is a photo of all of us. We (7) _____ (rest) half way up the pyramid!

A: Funny! Well, at least you (8) _____ (smile).

B: Yes, we (9) _____ (have) a good time.

C | Look at the photo and write three sentences using the present continuous tense. Read your sentences to your partner

1. _____

2. _____

3. _____

Language Function: Asking for Repetition

Here are some phrases you can use when you want someone to repeat something you didn't understand.

What?   *What did you say?*   *Excuse me?*   *Did you say . . . ?*

A | Read and listen to the conversations. Then <u>underline</u> the expressions that show when the speakers don't understand.
track 1-32

Conversation 1

A: What are you doing?

B: I'm reading a book on South Africa.

A: What did you say?

B: I'm reading a book on South Africa. I'm going to Cape Town next month.

Conversation 2

A: Do you want to have dinner now?

B: No, I'm planning my vacation.

A: Did you say you're planning your vacation?

B: Yes, I leave next week!

B | Practice the conversations from exercise **A** with a partner. Then switch roles and practice them again.

C | **Critical Thinking.** Work with a group of your classmates. Follow the instructions below.

Imagine you are on a vacation. Tell your classmates what you are doing on your vacation. Your classmates try to guess where you are. Your classmates can ask for repetition if they don't understand something.

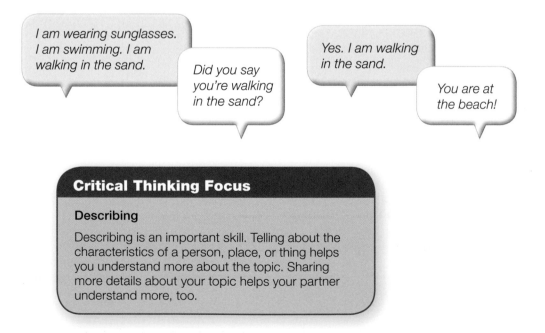

I am wearing sunglasses. I am swimming. I am walking in the sand.

Did you say you're walking in the sand?

Yes. I am walking in the sand.

You are at the beach!

Critical Thinking Focus

Describing

Describing is an important skill. Telling about the characteristics of a person, place, or thing helps you understand more about the topic. Sharing more details about your topic helps your partner understand more, too.

Choosing the Best Vacation

A | Look at these unusual destinations with a partner. Discuss what type of vacation each one is. Use descriptions from the box below. Write all the descriptions that apply in the chart.

adventurous	dangerous	incredible	relaxing	rough	special	typical
breathtaking	exciting	one of a kind	risky	secluded	thrilling	unusual

◄ Sightseeing in Antarctica

▲ Ballooning in Turkey   ▲ Kayaking in the Philippines

Vacation Destinations		
Turkey	Antarctica	Philippines

B | **Critical Thinking.** Think about each vacation in exercise **A**. Which vacation is best for you? Think about two people you know well. Which vacation is best for them?

C | Tell a partner about the vacation plans you have for you and your two friends.

D | **Collaboration.** Work with your partner to discuss which vacation is best for your teacher. Discuss his or her likes, dislikes, and personality and decide which of the three vacations is best.

E | **Presentation.** Share your vacation plan for your teacher with the class. Explain why you think this vacation is best for him/her. After all classmates share their ideas, the teacher tells you which vacation he/she chooses.

Blue Lagoon

▲ Tourists soaking in Blue Lagoon spa at Svartsengi
Geothermal Power Plant, Reykjanes Peninsula, Iceland

Before Viewing

A | Prior Knowledge. In this video, you will learn about an unusual destination in Iceland. When you think of Iceland, what words come to mind? Create a mind map with your words about Iceland. Share your ideas with a partner.

ice

Iceland

B | Predicting Content. Lesson **A** is about unusual natural places. Lesson **B** is about unusual manmade places. This video is about a spa that is both a natural and manmade destination. Before viewing, predict how this tourist destination is both natural and manmade.

Natural	Manmade

C | Using a Dictionary. Match each word to its definition. Use a dictionary to help you.

1. lagoon (n.) _____   a. to attract

2. giant (adj.) _____   b. a person who is visiting a place on vacation

3. lure (v.) _____   c. people who live in a particular place

4. healing powers (n.) _____   d. very large

5. tourist (n.) _____   e. feeling nervous

6. tense (adj.) _____   f. the ability to make healthy

7. locals (n.) _____   g. an area of shallow water separated from the sea

While Viewing

A | Checking Predictions. Watch the video and check your predictions in exercise **B** on page 72.

B | Watch the video again. Answer the questions.

1. How is the Blue Lagoon formed? Number the sentences in order (1 = first; 5 = last).

    _____ The water goes into the lava fields.

    _____ The plant pumps the water back out.

    _____ The plant uses the water to make energy.

    _____ The water forms a lagoon.

    _____ The power plant takes super heated water out of the ground.

2. Where is the lagoon located?

    a. In a power plant within a volcano

    b. Next to a power plant and surrounded by volcanoes and old lava fields

    c. Near a steamy lake

3. How many tourists visit the Blue Lagoon each year?

    a. 30,000　　　　　b. 130,000　　　　　c. 300,000

4. What are some of the benefits of the water in the Blue Lagoon?

    a. The water makes you feel giant and tense.

    b. The water makes you feel hungry and tired.

    c. The water makes you feel relaxed and young.

C | Using the Present Continuous. Watch the video again without the sound. With a partner, tell what the people are doing in the video.

> They are swimming.

After Viewing

A | Discussion. Form a group with two or three other students. Discuss the questions.

1. The soft blue-green water of the Blue Lagoon lures many people every year. What lures you to a vacation spot? (e.g., good shopping, natural beauty, adventure, historical sites)

2. Many people believe that the Blue Lagoon has natural healing powers. Do you believe in natural healing powers? Explain.

3. Is there a place in your country where people go for natural healing powers? Do the locals go there or are there more tourists?

> I don't think it is good to tell tourists about the locals' favorite places. The places are not special anymore.

B | Critical Thinking. Many locals don't like to tell the tourists about their favorite places. Is this good or bad? Explain your answer to a partner.

> I think it is good to tell tourists about the best places. Tourists bring money to our town.

track **1-33**

A | **Meaning from Context.** Look at the photos. Then read and listen to the descriptions. Notice the words in **blue**. These are words you will hear and use in Lesson **B**.

There are many breathtaking places on Earth. Some of them are **natural** places and others are **manmade attractions**. From very old to very modern, we **recommend** the following **spectacular** manmade destinations.

Manmade islands of Dubai

These are manmade islands off the coast of Dubai. They are several miles wide. One group of islands is in the shape of palm trees and another group is in the shape of a world map. They are resort islands. Many people visit them each year.

Petra, Jordan

This city is 2500 years old and is on many travelers' lists for unusual destinations. It is in the middle of the Jordanian desert. There are many beautiful temples[1] and monuments.[2] It is recommended for travelers seeking an unknown vacation spot.

Wat Rong Khun, Thailand

There are many temples in Thailand, but the Rong Khun, named The White Temple, is spectacular. It is just outside Chang Rai in northern Thailand. This unusual temple is all white. It has a **mix** of modern and old styles together.

SkyPark, Singapore

SkyPark is located on top of three tall buildings. It **overlooks** the beautiful city of Singapore. With restaurants, a large swimming pool, and a museum of modern art, there is something for everyone. The **view** is breathtaking!

[1] A **temple** is a building where people go to pray.

[2] A **monument** is a statue or building to remember an important person or event.

B | Match each word in **blue** from exercise **A** with its definition.

1. natural (adj.) _____
2. manmade (adj.) _____
3. attraction (n.) _____
4. recommend (v.) _____
5. spectacular (adj.) _____
6. view (n.) _____
7. mix (n.) _____
8. overlook (v.) _____

a. to look out on something
b. combination
c. an area that you can see
d. very exciting or impressive
e. not made by people
f. made by people
g. something interesting or fun to do
h. to suggest or advise

A | Read the sentences. Circle the correct word.

1. I like to go to manmade (attractions / overlooks). I like to see modern buildings.

2. I am standing on top of the mountain now. The (view / overlook) is breathtaking.

3. The mountains and rivers are (natural / manmade) attractions in this country.

4. This bridge (overlooks / mix) the lake. It is a breathtaking view.

5. I like a mix of (manmade / spectacular) and natural destinations.

6. That man (overlooks / recommends) the natural attractions. He says they are spectacular.

7. A(n) (mix / attraction) of old and modern is an interesting style.

8. The view from the top of the building is (spectacular / recommend).

B | **Discussion.** With a partner, discuss these questions.

1. Do you like natural or manmade attractions?
2. Describe a spectacular view.

▲ An ice sculpture at a festival in China

C | **Critical Thinking.** With a group of your classmates, think of natural and manmade attractions in your city, in your country, and around the world. Complete the chart. Share the attractions with the rest of the class.

Attractions			
	City	Country	World
Natural			
Manmade			

D | Did you visit any of the attractions you listed in the chart above? Share your experience with a partner. Do you recommend it?

I went to the Grand Canyon. The view was spectacular.

SkyPark in Singapore is beautiful. I recommend it.

Before Listening

 Predicting Content. You are going to listen to a conversation about a person's trip to an attraction. Look at the photo and discuss these questions with a partner.

Where do you think the attraction is? What kind of attraction do you think it is?
Is it manmade? Is it natural? What do you think the person will say about it?

Listening: A Group Conversation

 A | Checking Predictions. Listen to the conversation. Then look back at your answers from the Before Listening exercise. Were your predictions right?

track 1-34

B | Listening for the Main Idea. Read the question and answer choices. Then listen again and choose the correct answer.

track 1-34

What did Maria think about her trip to the ICEHOTEL?

a. It was a very cold, manmade attraction.

b. It was a good mix of a natural and manmade attraction.

c. It was secluded and relaxing.

C | Listening for Details. Listen again and circle the details from the story.

It's 200 km north of the Arctic Circle.	The restaurant serves only cold food.
You can only stay one night.	You sleep on reindeer skins.
There were 47 rooms this year.	The hotel is the same every year.
You don't need a hat or warm clothes.	The temperature stays between -5 and -8 degrees Celsius.
They serve you hot juice in the morning.	Maria recommends a one-week stay.

D | Making Inferences. Read the statements. Then listen again and circle **T** for *true* or **F** for *false*. The answers are not in the speaker's exact words. You need to think about what you hear.

1. This was Maria's second time at the ICEHOTEL.   **T**   **F**
2. Maria likes to go to unknown destinations.   **T**   **F**
3. The ICEHOTEL is dependent on the weather.   **T**   **F**
4. You need warm clothes inside the ICEHOTEL.   **T**   **F**

E | Compare your answers with a partner.

After Listening

Collaboration. Form a group with two or three other students. Create an unusual manmade attraction. Complete the chart and then share your idea with your classmates.

What is the name of the attraction?	What is the attraction?	Where is the attraction?	Who likes the attraction?

Pronunciation: Reduction of *-ing*

When people speak English quickly, they don't always pronounce every word fully. In fast speech, the *-ing* in the present continuous often gets reduced. Listen to the sentences. Pay attention to the reduction of the *-ing*.

Careful Speech	Fast Speech
I am looking at the view.	*I'm **lookin'** at the view.*
We are relaxing on the beach.	*We're **relaxin'** on the beach.*
They are eating breakfast.	*They're **eatin'** breakfast.*

With a partner, practice saying the sentences below. Reduce the *-ing* sound.

1. She's staying at the ICEHOTEL.
2. We are going on vacation.
3. They are walking on the bridge.
4. I'm seeing the attractions today.
5. He is getting away this weekend.

Grammar: The Present Continuous in Questions

Yes/No Questions	***Wh-*** Questions
Are you sleeping?	*What are you doing?*
Is he/she/it traveling?	*Why is she leaving?*
Are they relaxing?	*Where are they going?*

A | Write the words in the correct order.

1. planning / are / your / you / trip / Easter Island / to / ?

   _____

2. brother / where / your / is / on / vacation / going / ?

   _____

3. getting away / are / parents / your / ?

   _____

4. is / why / John / going / spot / a / secluded / to / ?

   _____

5. your / are / friends / train / riding / the / ?

   _____

6. plane / when / the / is / coming / ?

   _____

7. you / leaving / now / are / ?

   _____

8. relaxing / now / on / my / are / friends / beach / the / ?

   _____

🎧 track 1-36 **B** | Listen to the telephone conversation. <u>Underline</u> the present continuous questions and statements.

A: Hi, Keiko? It's Alex. Are you working now?

B: No, I'm taking my vacation this week.

A: Where are you?

B: I'm on Easter Island. I'm on a group tour with 15 other people.

A: Wow! Are you having a good time?

B: Yes, I'm learning a lot about the island and I'm having a lot of fun.

A: What are you doing right now?

B: I'm hiking up a big mountain.

A: Are you seeing beautiful views?

B: Yes, I'm standing on a bridge that overlooks the island's famous statues. It's a spectacular view!

👥 **C** | Practice the conversation from exercise **B** with a partner.

D | Role-Playing. With a partner, read the scenario for the role play. Complete the role play dialog and then practice it with your partner. Perform the role play for the class.

Role play scenario: You are on vacation. Your friend calls. Create a telephone conversation.

A: Hi. (1) _____ (name).

B: Oh, hi (2) _____ (name).

A: Where are you?

B: I'm on vacation. I'm in (3) _____.

A: Oh! What are you doing now?

B: (4) _____.

A: Really?

B: Yes, and I'm also (5) _____.

A: (6) _____ (have a good time)?

B: (7) _____.

A: Well, have fun!

B: Thanks for calling.

E | Discussion. Form a group with two or three other students. Discuss the questions.

1. Do you like to take vacations on your own or with other people? Explain.

2. What are the good points (**pros**) and bad points (**cons**) of taking a group tour? Write your ideas in the chart.

> **Student to Student**
>
> **Working Together**
>
> Pair work and group work are common classroom activities. Here are some expressions you can use when working with other people.
>
> *Let's work together.*   *Do you want to work together?*
> *Let's get started.*   *We need one more idea.*

Taking a Group Tour	
Pros	Cons

ENGAGE: Giving an Individual Presentation

In this section, you are going to think about the type of vacations you like and how you like to spend your time on vacation. You will create a graph with these ideas and then give a presentation to the rest of the class about your preferences.

▲ Seeing historical sites ▲ Relaxing ▲ Doing activities

A | Critical Thinking. On vacation, how much time do you like to relax, see historical sites, or do activities? Look at the sample pie chart. Then complete the blank chart with your own information.

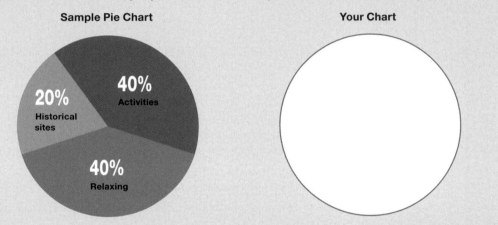

Sample Pie Chart

- 40% Activities
- 20% Historical sites
- 40% Relaxing

Your Chart

B | Planning a Presentation. Look at the sample presentation below based on the sample chart above. Replace the underlined words with your own information.

Hello. I want to tell you how I like to spend my time on vacation. On vacations, I like to <u>do many things</u>. As we can see from my graph, <u>20 percent of the time I like to see historical sites</u>. I like to learn a little about the place I am visiting. Looking at my graph, <u>40 percent of the time I like to do activities</u>. I like to <u>go to natural attractions and hike or bike</u>. The graph shows that the last <u>40 percent of my vacation, I like to relax. I have such a busy schedule at home. It is nice to have time to relax on my vacation</u>. Are there any questions?

C | Practicing your Presentation. Copy your graph on a bigger piece of paper. Practice pointing to the graph when giving your presentation.

D | Presentation. Give your presentation to the class. Remember to point to your graph.

Presentation Skills: Using Graphics

Using graphics in a presentation helps your audience understand your topic more. Say these phrases when using graphics.

This graph shows . . .   *As we can see from this graph . . .*

Our Changing World

ACADEMIC PATI IWAYS

Lesson A: Listening to a Lecture
            Discussing Traditions
Lesson B: Listening to a Short Documentary
            Presenting to a Small Group

Think and Discuss

1. Look at the photo. What is the man doing?

2. Does this look like something people do today, a long time ago, or both? Explain.

▲ Buddhist monk Shi Dejian practices kung fu at the mountaintop retreat he has spent 15 years building.

Exploring the Theme:
Our Changing World

Look at the photos and read the captions and the information. Then discuss the questions.

1. Compare the two photos of Manhattan Island, New York. How did the island change?

2. How have your family's traditions (your beliefs and customs) changed since you were young?

3. Do you think change is good? Explain.

What does *change* mean to you? If we look, we can see changes in the style of clothes we wear, the music we listen to, and the way we dance. We can see changes in the cities we live in and the way we shop. But there are some changes that are harder to see, for example, changes in traditions. Life is full of changes. What changes do you see around you?

▲ Manhattan Island, New York, as it could have looked before 1609.

▼ Manhattan Island, New York, as it looks today.

A | **Using a Dictionary.** Listen and check (✓) the words you already know. Use a dictionary to help you with any new words. These are words you will hear and use in Lesson **A**.

track 2-01

- ☐ become (v.)
- ☐ competition (n.)
- ☐ develop (v.)
- ☐ entertainment (n.)
- ☐ hope (v.)
- ☐ practice (v.)
- ☐ skill (n.)
- ☐ young (adj.)

B | Match each word with its definition.

1. become _____
2. competition _____
3. hope _____
4. skill _____

a. a contest or activity in which people try to win
b. to want or wish for something
c. a special ability to do something well
d. to turn into, come to be

C | **Meaning from Context.** Read and listen to the article. Notice the words in **blue**. Then write a word next to its definition below.

track 2-02

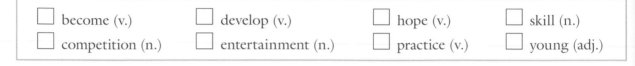

Shaolin Kung Fu Master: Hu Zhengsheng

When Hu Zhengsheng was a **young** boy, he loved to watch kung fu films. He saw kung fu as a form of **entertainment**. Hu went to Shaolin Temple[1] when he was 11 years old. He **became** a servant[2] to one of the teachers. He **practiced** martial arts[3] for many years and learned the movements for self-defense and good health.

Hu started a small school. Today his school has 200 students. He teaches the students traditional Shaolin kung fu. His students sleep in cold rooms. Every day they **practice** kung fu very early in the morning even in very cold weather. It is hard, but Hu knows this will help his students **develop** the **skills** they need in life. It will also help them **become** good at Shaolin kung fu.

1. _____ to do something to get better
2. _____ not old
3. _____ performances or activities that give people pleasure
4. _____ to grow or change over time

---

[1] **Shaolin Temple** is a Buddhist building of worship in China that is associated with Shaolin kung fu.

[2] A **servant** is a person who works for someone else.

[3] **Martial arts** are special exercises and movements that are practiced for self-defense, competition, physical and mental health, and spiritual development.

USING VOCABULARY

A | **Group Discussion.** Read the article in exercise **C** on page 84 again. Form a group with two or three students. Discuss the questions.

1. What two things did you learn about Hu Zhengsheng?
2. Do you think his school is hard or easy?
3. Do you think Hu likes his work? Explain.

B | Read and listen to the article. Then fill in each blank with a word from the box. Use each word only once. Then check your answers with a partner.

track **2-03**

competitions	hope	practice	skills

What is Shaolin kung fu? Where did it come from? There is an old story in China. It says that many years ago the monks[4] at Shaolin Temple learned special exercises. These exercises were hard and took a lot of practice. Later, the monks named these exercises "kung fu." The monks used kung fu to defend themselves from people who wanted to fight them.

Today, monks still (1) _____ kung fu, but they do not use it to fight. Many young boys and girls study kung fu near the Shaolin Temple. They are learning (2) _____ that will help them find good jobs. Some students (3) _____ to become movie stars. Some students want to win kickboxing (4) _____. In the past, kung fu was used for war, but today it is a form of entertainment.

▲ Shaolin Kung Fu: The Changing World of Martial Arts

C | Work with a partner. Read the conversation and fill in each blank with a word from the box. Then practice the conversation.

competitions	practice	skills	young

A: Hi, Lucas! I'm going to the library. Do you want to come?

B: No, I can't. I have to (1) _____ kung fu today.

A: Oh! How long have you been practicing kung fu?

B: Since I was a (2) _____ boy.

A: Do you do martial arts (3) _____?

B: Yes, I do! I like to compete. Martial arts teaches you many different (4) _____.

[4] A **monk** is a religious person.

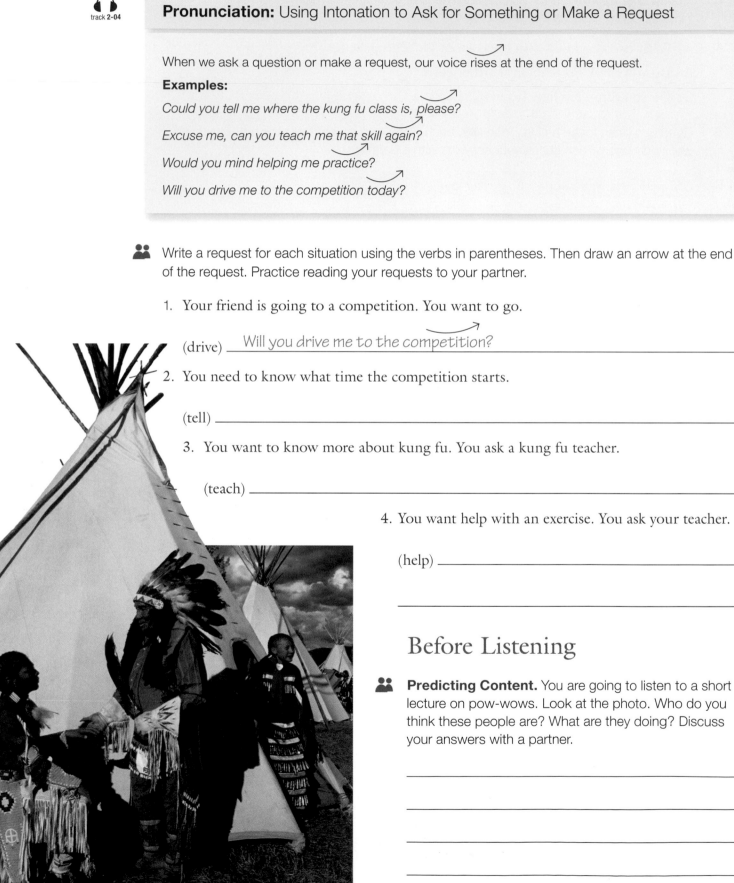

track 2-04

Pronunciation: Using Intonation to Ask for Something or Make a Request

When we ask a question or make a request, our voice rises at the end of the request.

Examples:

Could you tell me where the kung fu class is, please?

Excuse me, can you teach me that skill again?

Would you mind helping me practice?

Will you drive me to the competition today?

👥 Write a request for each situation using the verbs in parentheses. Then draw an arrow at the end of the request. Practice reading your requests to your partner.

1. Your friend is going to a competition. You want to go.

   (drive) _Will you drive me to the competition?_

2. You need to know what time the competition starts.

   (tell) _____?

3. You want to know more about kung fu. You ask a kung fu teacher.

   (teach) _____?

4. You want help with an exercise. You ask your teacher.

   (help) _____

   _____?

Before Listening

👥 **Predicting Content.** You are going to listen to a short lecture on pow-wows. Look at the photo. Who do you think these people are? What are they doing? Discuss your answers with a partner.

_____

_____

_____

_____

Listening: A Lecture

A | Listening for the Main Idea. Listen to the lecture. Check (✓) the main idea of the conversation.

☐ Pow-wows are fun.

☐ Traditions change over time.

☐ Native Americans dance and sing at pow-wows.

B | Listening for Details. Listen to the lecture again and circle the correct answer.

1. A pow-wow is a _____ tradition.
   a. Japanese   b. French   c. Native American

2. An important tradition at a pow-wow is _____.
   a. eating   b. dancing   c. practicing

3. Today, you can see men and women playing _____ at a pow-wow.
   a. music   b. sports   c. competition

C | Checking Predictions. Look back at the predictions you made on page 86. Then listen to the lecture again. Were your predictions correct?

After Listening

Self-Reflection. Discuss these questions with a partner.

1. Do you think traditional celebrations are important? Why, or why not?

2. What traditions do you celebrate?

3. How have your traditions changed over time?

Grammar: The Simple Past Tense

We use the simple past tense to talk about completed actions in the past.

Examples: I **traveled** to many countries last year.
Last night, I **talked** to my mother on the phone.

To form the simple past tense with regular verbs, add -ed.

Examples: listen – listen**ed**   walk – walk**ed**

To form the simple past tense with regular verbs that end in -e, add -d.

Examples: hope – hope**d**   love – love**d**

To form the simple past tense with regular verbs that end in -y, remove the -y and add -ied.

Examples: carry – carr**ied**   hurry – hurr**ied**

Many verbs are irregular in the simple past tense.

Examples: think – thought   go – went

track **2-06**
Read and listen to the following conversation. Then fill in each blank with the simple past tense of a verb from the box.

| bake | help | learn | like | think | want | work |

A: Why did you start your own pastry shop?

B: I (1) _____ to continue the tradition of baking French pastry. I (2) _____ the younger generation was eating too much fast food. I wanted them to eat traditional dessert such as our French pastries.

A: Where did you learn to bake French pastries?

B: Oh! I (3) _____ my father when I was young. I (4) _____ in his pastry shop.

A: How long did you work in his pastry shop?

B: Well, let's see . . . I (5) _____ with my father for ten years.

A: Wow! Why so long?

B: I (6) _____ working in the shop and talking to different people. I (7) _____ a lot while I was there.

A: Annie, what you have done is very important. People like you keep our traditions for the next generation.

B: Thanks! I hope so!

Language Function: Past Tense Time Expressions

When we talk about a past event, we use past tense time expressions.

Example: *Yesterday* *we went to a pow-wow.*

Here are some common past tense time expressions you can use to talk about a past event.

yesterday	*last*	*night* *week* *month* *year* *Monday, Tuesday, etc.*	*one day* *two weeks* *three months* *many years*	*ago*

A | Write sentences about past events. Then read your sentences to a partner.

1. Yesterday _____.

2. Last night _____.

3. Two weeks ago _____.

4. Last Saturday _____.

B | Circle the correct time expression that best completes the sentence. Then listen to the passage and check your answers. Take turns reading the passage with your partner.
track 2-07

The clothes people wear **1.** (last year / today) are different from the
clothes in the past. **2.** (Many years ago / Now), the clothes looked much
different. For example, in the 1900s, women wore long dresses and
hats. It is interesting to see how the clothes we wear change over time.
Change is a part of our lives. It occurs in our traditions, clothes, work,
and transportation. What we think is beautiful **3.** (last week / today) we
might not think is beautiful

4. (three months ago /
tomorrow). What do you think
clothes will look like in the
future? Will the clothes of
tomorrow look like the clothes
of **5.** (last night / today)?

C | With a partner, compare the
clothes in the two photos. How
are they the same? How are they
different?

D | Read the conversation. Fill in each blank with the simple present or simple past form of the verb in parentheses. Then practice the conversation with your partner.

A: Maryam, I know you are from Dubai. What is Dubai like?

B: Well, Dubai is a city of change!

A: What do you mean?

B: Many years ago, Dubai was a small fishing and trading village in the Persian Gulf. But today, it is a beautiful city. It is famous for its very tall buildings. People (1) _____ (shop) in amazing shopping malls. It is an international city. People from different countries (2) _____ (live) and (3) _____ (work) in Dubai.

A: I have a friend who (4) _____ (live) in Dubai four years ago. He (5) _____ (love) meeting people from so many different countries there. My friend said he (6) _____ (enjoy) his stay. But he (7) _____ (notice) many changes.

B: I think your friend is right. For example, today you can (8) _____ (see) fast-food restaurants everywhere. Younger people from Dubai now (9) _____ (eat) a lot of fast food.

A: Hmmm. That is interesting, but it's also sad.

B: I (10) _____ (know), but it is hard to stop change.

E | Look at the photo. Answer the questions. Compare your answers with a partner.

1. What do you notice about the buildings in Dubai today?

   _____

   _____

2. Do you think people lived a more quiet life in old Dubai? Why, or why not?

   _____

3. Dubai today is much bigger and more modern than it used to be. Do you think the lifestyle changed? How?

   _____

F | **Discussion.** In a group, discuss how your town or city changed. Does it have more buildings, parks, streets, cars? Did the people change? How?

Discussing Traditions

A | **Self-Reflection.** Think of a tradition from your culture. It could be a wedding tradition, holiday tradition, or family tradition. Then complete the chart below with your answers.

Questions	My Answers	My Partner's Answers
1. What is the name of the tradition or celebration?		
2. Which country is it celebrated in?		
3. Is it celebrated every year?		
4. What do you do?		
5. Do you wear special clothes?		
6. Who celebrates with you?		
7. Do you eat traditional food? What is it?		
8. Is this tradition important? Why?		

B | With a partner, ask and answer the questions from exercise **A**. Complete the chart with your partner's answers then talk about your answers.

C | **Critical Thinking.** Form a group and discuss the questions.

1. Do you think it is important to keep old traditions? Explain.
2. Talk about your charts. Do you have the same traditions?
3. Do you have any traditional sports or games in your culture?

POW-WOWS

Before Viewing

A | **Critical Thinking.** Discuss these questions with a partner.

1. What do you remember about pow-wows from Lesson **A** of this unit?

2. In Lesson **A**, you learned that changes happen in our traditions, the clothes we wear, and the places we live. Do you think change is necessary?

B | **Using a Dictionary.** Read and listen to the information. Then use your dictionary to help you with the underlined words.

This video shows a pow-wow in South Dakota. You see Native Americans dancing. You hear Native Americans singing to drums. You also listen to a Native American named Buck Spotted Tail from the Sioux <u>reservation</u> talk. He talks about how he learned to dance like his <u>ancestors</u>. He also tells how he <u>gradually</u> changed the way he dances to a more <u>contemporary</u> style. Buck Spotted Tail talks about why it is important for Native American families to get together at pow-wows. It is where they have fun and learn to sing and dance. Native Americans also learn more about their traditions at pow-wows. Buck Spotted Tail says that a pow-wow is a way to bring people together in a big celebration.

C | Write each underlined word from exercise **B** next to its definition below.

1. _____ (n.) people in your family who lived before you
2. _____ (adj.) modern
3. _____ (n.) an area of land for Native Americans
4. _____ (adv.) slowly

While Viewing

A | Watch the video. Then circle **T** for *true* or **F** for *false*.

1. Buck Spotted Tail is from the Rosebud Sioux reservation.	**T**	**F**
2. He does not have an Indian name.	**T**	**F**
3. He started dancing when he was six.	**T**	**F**
4. He changed the way he danced.	**T**	**F**

B | Watch the video again. Check (✓) the things people do at pow-wows.

☐ sing ☐ dance ☐ play games ☐ meet different families

After Viewing

Discussion. With a partner, discuss the following questions.

1. Is it important for families to get together to celebrate traditions? Explain.
2. Is music important in celebrations? Explain.
3. Is dancing important in celebrations? Explain.

A | **Meaning from Context.** Read and listen to the news article about saving energy in Pakistan. Notice the words in **blue**. These are words you will hear and use in Lesson **B**.

track 2-09

A NEED FOR LIFESTYLE CHANGE

With 165 million people in Pakistan, there is a shortage of electricity. During the day, the electricity often goes out. Sometimes the electricity goes out for 12 hours or more! The government is asking shops to close early to save energy. Shop owners are not happy. They say customers do not want to shop in the day when there is no electricity because it is too hot. The government also has new rules for weddings and banks. Pakistani wedding celebrations must finish earlier instead of ending after midnight. Government offices and banks now have a two-day weekend, instead of a one-day weekend.

A CHANGE IN LIFESTYLE MEANS MORE ENERGY

Because of the new rules, people are slowly changing their habits. They are adapting to a new lifestyle. For example, now they shop before 8:00 P.M. Celebrations end earlier and people are more careful of how they use electricity. This change of lifestyle is very important and has helped the government save energy.

B | **Using a Dictionary.** Check (✓) the words you already know or understand from the context of exercise **A**. Then use a dictionary to help you with any new words.

☐ adapt (v.)	☐ electricity (n.)	☐ habit (n.)	☐ rule (n.)
☐ customer (n.)	☐ energy (n.)	☐ lifestyle (n.)	☐ shortage (n.)

C | Complete each sentence with a word from exercise **B**.

1. The Pakistani government made a new _____ to save energy.

2. As a _____, I like to shop in the evening when it is cooler.

3. My roommate has a bad _____ of leaving the lights on when she's not home.

A | Complete each sentence with a word from the box.

adapted	electricity	lifestyle	rules	shortage

1. Every society has _____ that people must obey.

2. Many countries have a _____ of water in the summer.

3. When we move to a new country, it is sometimes necessary to change our _____.

4. People in Pakistan _____ to a new way of living.

5. Living without _____ is difficult.

B | Read the interview. Circle the correct word in **blue**.

Interviewer: Why are shop owners so unhappy about the new **1.** (**rules** / **customers**)?

Shop owner: Well, we have to close earlier at night to save **2.** (**habit** / **energy**) and shop owners lose a lot of business.

Interviewer: Why can't people shop earlier in the day?

Shop owner: Because it is too hot. When the **3.** (**lifestyle** / **electricity**) goes out during the day, there is no air conditioning!

Interviewer: I see! So, the electricity **4.** (**shortage** / **lifestyle**) is changing the time people want to shop.

Shop owner: Yes. **5.** (**Customers** / **Habits**) like to shop at night when the weather is cooler.

Interviewer: Do you think people will **6.** (**lifestyle** / **adapt**) to this new way of shopping?

Shop owner: It is hard to say. But, yes, I think we must change our **7.** (**energy** / **lifestyle**) because we have no choice.

C | **Critical Thinking.** Discuss the questions with your partner.

1. What are two other ways Pakistanis can save **energy**?

2. What are some ways you can save **energy**?

3. Do you think changing your **lifestyle** is easy to do? Explain.

A traditional candlelit ▶ wedding in Pakistan

Pronunciation: The Intonation of *Wh-* Questions

track 2-10

When we ask a question with *what, when, where,* and *why,* the speaker's voice first rises and then falls at the end of the sentence.

What do customers want?

When do shop owners close their shops?

Where is the shortage of electricity?

Why don't customers like to shop in the day?

track 2-11

A | Listen to the following conversation. Draw an arrow where you hear the voice rise and fall in the *Wh-* questions. Then practice the conversation with a partner.

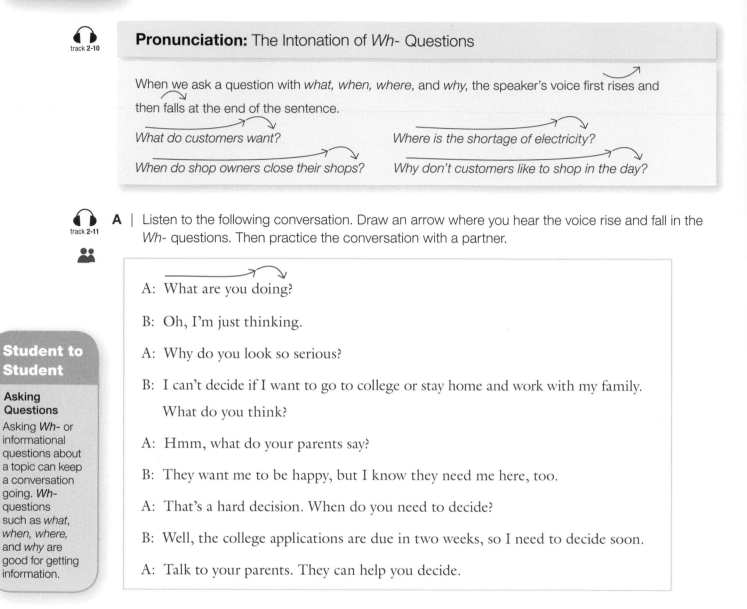

A: What are you doing?

B: Oh, I'm just thinking.

A: Why do you look so serious?

B: I can't decide if I want to go to college or stay home and work with my family. What do you think?

A: Hmm, what do your parents say?

B: They want me to be happy, but I know they need me here, too.

A: That's a hard decision. When do you need to decide?

B: Well, the college applications are due in two weeks, so I need to decide soon.

A: Talk to your parents. They can help you decide.

Student to Student

Asking Questions

Asking *Wh-* or informational questions about a topic can keep a conversation going. *Wh-* questions such as *what, when, where,* and *why* are good for getting information.

B | Read the answers. Then write the *Wh-* questions.

1. Q: _When do people shop in Pakistan now?_

   A: _People shop in the day in Pakistan now._

2. Q: _____

   A: _The shortage of electricity is in Pakistan._

3. Q: _____

   A: _Banks have a two-day weekend to save energy._

4. Q: _____

   A: _People are changing their habits._

C | Practice reading the questions and answers in exercise **A** with a partner.

Before Listening

Read the introduction then read the statements below. Circle **T** for *true* or **F** for *false*.

Ella-Li Spik is a Sami. The Sami are a small group of people who live in Sweden. They herd[5] reindeer. Ella-Li grew up herding reindeer. But things are changing for the Sami. Ella-Li is part of a new generation that wants to attend college. "I want to explore the world," she says, "but I always want reindeer to be part of my life."

1. Ella-Li Spik is Swedish.	T	F
2. She grew up in the city.	T	F
3. She wants to go to college.	T	F
4. She doesn't like reindeer.	T	F

Critical Thinking Focus

Listening for the Main Idea

When you listen to a conversation, lecture, or documentary, you can listen for different types of information. Listening for key words or key phrases can help you understand the main idea of a topic. For example, if you hear the following key words in a sentence, "Paris," "trip," "last year," you can guess that the person is speaking about a trip to Paris last year.

Listening: A Short Documentary

A | **Listening for the Main Idea.** Read the sentences. Listen to the documentary and choose the correct answer.

track 2-12

a. The documentary is about Sami lifestyle.

b. The documentary is about reindeer.

c. The documentary is about the changing lifestyle of Samis.

B | **Listening for Details.** Listen again. Use words from the box to fill in the blanks.

track 2-12

vehicles	traditions	changing	animals

1. Many years ago, the herders followed the fast _____ on foot or wooden skis.

2. The Sami herders use special _____ and snowmobiles to move large herds of reindeer.

3. The Sami lifestyle is _____.

4. If reindeer herding disappears, Sami _____ may disappear, too.

After Listening

Critical Thinking. With a partner, discuss how you think older people feel about changes in traditions and lifestyles.

---

[5] To **herd** means to bring people or animals together in a large group.

track **2-13**

A | Read and listen to a short lecture about how and why people in Venice, Italy, are changing their lifestyles.

Venice, Italy, is changing. For hundreds of years, Venice has been flooding. But the flooding is getting worse. When it floods, water is everywhere! As a result, Venetians have made many changes to their lifestyles. First of all, every Venetian has boots in his or her closet. Also, when it floods, people have learned to walk on the high footpaths that are set up in the city. Venetians use boat timetables instead of bus timetables. And, when they want to move from their apartments, they do not use trucks to move their furniture—instead they use boats. Unfortunately, many people are leaving Venice. They cannot adapt to the flooding and lifestyle changes.

◄ A woman walks the flooded streets of Venice.

B | **Discussion.** In a small group, discuss the questions below.

1. What did you learn about Venice?

2. How are people in Venice changing their lifestyle?

3. Venice, Italy, is an island. What do you think will happen to it?

Grammar: The Simple Present vs. the Simple Past Tense of the Verb *Be*

Present		Past	
I *am*		I *was*	
You *are*		You *were*	
He *is*		He *was*	
She *is*	in Tokyo today.	She *was*	in Tokyo yesterday.
It *is*		It *was*	
We *are*		We *were*	
They *are*		They *were*	

A | Complete the conversation using either the simple present or the simple past of the verb *to be*.

A: I (1) _____ in San Francisco last week.

B: Why did you go there?

A: My family lives there and I wanted to visit them.

B: Wow! You (2) _____ so lucky! San Francisco

(3) _____ such an interesting city. I

(4) _____ there two years ago. I remember how beautiful

the Golden Gate Bridge (5) _____.

A: I know! I love San Francisco! But things (6) _____

different. The city has changed.

B: How has it changed?

A: Well, some of the older buildings (7) _____ not there.

People want to build newer and safer homes. They want homes that will

not fall during an earthquake.[6]

B: Did you see any other changes?

A: Yes. San Francisco is more international. There (8) _____

more people from all over the world living in San Francisco now.

B: So, San Francisco really has changed in many ways.

A: Yes, it has. But there (9) _____ one thing that

(10) _____ still the same—the Golden Gate Bridge!

I hope it never changes.

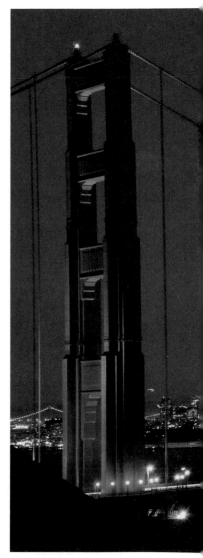

B | Listen to the conversation and check your answers. Then practice reading the conversation with a partner.

track 2-14

C | **Discussion.** With your partner, discuss what your country was famous for in the past. Is it still famous for this today?

[6] An **earthquake** is when the ground shakes because the Earth's surface is moving.

ENGAGE: Presenting to a Small Group

In this section, you are going to give a presentation to a small group about a tradition in your culture that is changing.

Presentation Skills: Presenting to a Small Group

When presenting to a small group, it is important to follow a few steps:

- Learn as much as you can about your topic.
- Know how much time you have.
- Be organized—your presentation needs an introduction, a middle, and an end.
- Write important information on small note cards (but do not read them).
- Speak clearly.
- Include posters or pictures about your topic.
- Practice your presentation at home.

A | **Organizing Ideas.** You are going to speak to a group of students about a tradition in your culture that is changing. Answer the following questions to organize your presentation.

Topic: _____

Describe the tradition: _____

Why is this tradition important in your culture? _____

_____

Is this tradition practiced only in your culture? If no, where else is it practiced?

_____

What changes do you see in this tradition? _____

_____

Why is it changing? _____

_____

Will you keep this tradition in your family? Why, or why not? _____

_____

B | **Practice Your Presentation.** Work with a partner. Take turns practicing your presentations. Listen to suggestions from your partner and make any needed changes.

C | **Presentation.** Give your presentation to a small group of students.

Facing Challenges

ACADEMIC PATHWAYS

Lesson A: Listening to a Presentation
Talking about the Past
Lesson B: Listening to a Conversation
Presenting from Notes

Think and Discuss

1. Look at the photo and read the caption. Describe what you see.

2. Do you think it is easy or difficult to be a scientist? Explain.

3. What do you think is the most difficult part of studying sequoia trees?

◄ A scientist studies sequoia trees from bottom to top.

Exploring the Theme: Facing Challenges

Look at the photos and read the captions. Then discuss the questions.

1. What does the word *challenge* mean?

2. Do you think it is more challenging to work with people or animals?

3. Which one of these jobs do you think is more challenging? Discuss.

4. Do we only have challenges at work? Explain.

▲ A repair person working on a radio tower

▲ Firefighters putting out a fire

▲ Pilots in the cockpit of an aircraft

▲ Joel Sartore takes a photograph of a baby caiman.

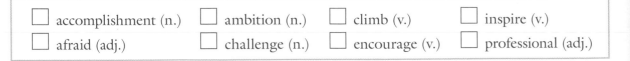
🎧 **A** | **Using a Dictionary.** Listen and check (✓) the words you already know. Then use a dictionary
track **2-15**   to help you with any new words. These are words you will hear and use in Lesson **A**.

☐ accomplishment (n.)   ☐ ambition (n.)   ☐ climb (v.)   ☐ inspire (v.)
☐ afraid (adj.)   ☐ challenge (n.)   ☐ encourage (v.)   ☐ professional (adj.)

B | Match each word from exercise **A** with its definition.

1. professional _____
2. ambition _____
3. accomplishment _____
4. encourage _____

a. to give someone hope or confidence
b. something special that has been done or achieved
c. a strong wish or desire to do something special
d. relating to a person's work, especially work that requires special training

C | Write one word from exercise **A** next to its definition.

1. _____ something new and difficult which takes a lot of effort to do
2. _____ to give someone new ideas and a strong feeling of excitement
3. _____ to move towards the top of something
4. _____ feeling fear that something bad will happen

🎧 **D** | **Meaning from Context.** Read and listen to the article. Notice the words in **blue**.
track **2-16**

Blind Ambition

Erik Weihenmayer lost his vision when he was 13 years old. He did not let being blind stop him from learning how to ski, mountain bike, and **climb** mountains. Erik became a **professional** athlete and continued his education. He became an elementary school teacher. He taught classes with up to 30 students in them. His other **accomplishments** include climbing the tallest mountains in all seven continents. He even climbed Mount Everest! He has **inspired** and guided blind Tibetan teenagers to 21,500 feet on Mount Everest. Erik has also led both blind and sighted students on hikes through the Andes. Erik must be well prepared and in good physical shape to achieve his **ambitions**. He is also a motivational speaker who **encourages** others and is successful because he is not **afraid** of any **challenge**.

A | Complete the conversation with words from the box. Use each word only once. Then listen and check your answers.

accomplishments	afraid	ambition	challenges
climbing	encourage	inspire	professional

A: Did you read the article on Erik Weihenmayer? Isn't he a fascinating person?

B: Yes, he really is! Imagine being blind and (1) _____ a mountain!

A: Even for people who can see, climbing a mountain is very difficult.

B: You know, I was really surprised to learn that he is also a teacher and a

(2) _____ athlete.

A: People like Erik really (3) _____ people all around the world. Did you know that

he is not the only person with a disability who has done amazing things?

B: Yes! I read about Helen Keller in school. She was blind, deaf, and could not speak. Helen Keller

became famous because of all the (4) _____ she had in her lifetime.

A. Right! But people who have disabilities are not the only people who face (5) _____.

We all have difficulties in our lives. We face challenges at home, at work, at school,

and in relationships.

B: I agree. Do you think challenges are good for us?

A: Yes, I do. I think if a person is not (6) _____ and has (7) _____,

then he or she can overcome most of life's challenges. I believe that challenges make us stronger.

B: You are so right! I think that people like Erik Weihenmayer

and Helen Keller really (8) _____ others to

be brave and face life's challenges and never give up!

B | Practice the conversation in exercise **A** with a partner. Then switch roles and practice it again.

C | **Discussion.** Look at the photo and read the caption. Then discuss the questions with your partner.

1. What **challenges** might this zoo director have working with animals?

2. Do you think he enjoys his work? Why, or why not?

3. Do you think orangutans are a **challenge** to work with? Why, or why not? Why, or why not.

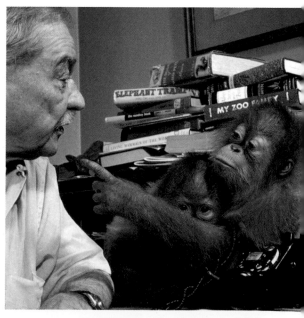

A zoo director communicating with orangutans ▶

Before Listening

 Predicting Content. Look at the photo. Answer the questions with a partner.

1. What is the man climbing?

2. Does this mountain look dangerous? Explain.

3. What challenges does a blind person have climbing a mountain?

4. What challenges does a person with one leg have climbing a mountain?

Listening: A Presentation

track 2-18

A | **Listening for Main Ideas.** Listen and choose the main idea of the presentation.

1. Erik loves climbing.

2. It is important to be prepared before facing a challenge.

3. Chad is not afraid of climbing.

track 2-18

B | **Listening for Details.** Listen again. Check (✓) the details that you hear. Then check your answers with a partner.

1. ☐ Both Erik and Chad are very active.

2. ☐ Chad listened to music when he climbed Bridal Veil Falls.

3. ☐ Erik is a teacher.

4. ☐ Erik was hit on the shoulder with a piece of ice while climbing.

5. ☐ Chad uses a special prosthesis[1] to climb.

track 2-18

C | **Checking Predictions.** Look back at the predictions you made at the top of the page. Then listen to the lecture again. Were your predictions correct?

[1] A **prosthesis** is an artificial hand, arm, or leg.

After Listening

A | Making Inferences. Read the statements and circle **T** for *true* or **F** for *false*.

1.	Erik enjoys challenges.	T	F
2.	Ice climbing can be dangerous.	T	F
3.	Bridal Veil Falls can only be climbed in the winter.	T	F
4.	Erik will not continue his adventures.	T	F

B | Role-Playing. Form a group with two or three other students. Interview each other and fill in the chart. Start your interview by saying, "Hi! I'd like to ask a few questions about the challenges of being a student."

Questions	Student 1	Student 2
How long have you been a student?		
What is the most challenging part of being a student?		
What are some challenges a teacher might have teaching students?		

C | Self-Reflection. Discuss the questions with a partner.

1. What is the most difficult job you can think of?
2. Why do you think the job is so challenging?
3. How do challenges make us stronger?

Pronunciation: The Simple Past Tense *-ed* Endings

track 2-19

Regular verbs in the simple past tense that end in -ed have three different pronunciations. In this section, we will learn about the /d/ sound.

-ed has a /d/ sound after these final sounds: /b/, /g/, /l/, /m/, /n/, /r/, /v/, /w/, /y/, or /z/

Examples: *plan* ➡ *plan**ed*** ➡ *plan/**d***/
          live ➡ *liv**ed*** ➡ *live/**d***/

track 2-20

Listen and repeat the words you hear.

1. inspired	4. climbed	7. encouraged
2. allowed	5. challenged	8. enjoyed
3. answered	6. cleaned	9. listened

Language Function: Expressing Difficulty with Something

There are many expressions we use to talk about challenges in the present or past.

Example: I **had a hard time** doing my homework.

Present Tense		Past Tense	
I have a hard time **It is difficult** **It is challenging**	} making a decision.	**I had a hard time** **It was difficult** **It was challenging**	} making a decision.

A | Circle the phrase that best completes the sentences. Then read your sentences to a partner.

1. When Soichiro Honda was younger, he (has a hard time / had a hard time) finding a job as an engineer. He went on to start his own business, Honda Motor Company.

2. For Walt Disney, it (is challenging / was challenging) starting a successful business. He started many businesses, but they did not succeed. Finally, he started Disneyland.

3. At first, it (is difficult / was difficult) finding a publisher[2] for J.K. Rowling's book *Harry Potter and the Sorcerer's Stone*.

B | Complete the following sentences. Then compare your answers with a small group.

1. When I was younger, I __had a hard time riding a bike__ .

2. I thought _____ .

3. Now that I am older, I think it is _____ .

4. Many students think that _____ .

C | **Collaboration.** Look at the photo. With your partner, make a list of challenges for people living in crowded cities. Then, write sentences. Start each sentence with an expression from the Language Function box.

> It is difficult commuting to work in a crowded city.

[2] A **publisher** is a company that prints books.

Grammar: Irregular Past Tense Verbs

Verbs are irregular if the past tense form of the verb does not end in -ed.
The following is a list of some irregular past tense verbs:

Base Form	Past Tense	Base Form	Past Tense
be	was/were	go	went
become	became	have	had
begin	began	know	knew
come	came	lose	lost
do	did	make	made
give	gave	write	wrote

A | Fill in each blank with the simple past tense of the verb in parentheses. Practice reading the sentences with a partner.

1. _____ (do) you get the job you wanted?

2. It _____ (be) challenging saving money for college lat year.

3. She _____ (go) to school to study science.

4. The teacher _____ (give) a lecture on how to face challenges as a student.

B | **Group Discussion.** With a small group, discuss the following questions. Use phrases from the Student to Student box so everyone has a turn speaking.

1. What are some challenges you faced when you started learning English?

2. Do you think everyone faces the same challenges in life?

C | Read exercise **B** on page 108 again. Answer the questions using past tense verbs from the Grammar box above. Then ask the questions to two other students. Remember to take turns speaking.

1. Was it difficult for J.K. Rowling to get her book published?

   _____

2. Did the challenges of getting her first book published stop her from writing more books?

   _____

3. Did Soichiro Honda have a hard time finding a job as an engineer?

   _____

4. Did he finally become a successful businessman?

   _____

> ### Student to Student
>
> **Taking Turns**
>
> When you are having a group discussion, taking turns can help make sure each person gets to talk. Here are some phrases you can use for taking turns:
>
> *Do you agree?*
>
> *What do you think?*
>
> *Do you want to say something?*
>
> *Your turn.*

track **2-21**

D | Read and listen to the following short story. Underline all the past tense verbs.

World Famous   Deaf Musician Inspires All Artists

Evelyn Glennie is a famous percussionist[3] and composer.[4] Like every musician, Evelyn has a challenging job. As a young musician, she spent hours and hours practicing and learning different musical instruments. And, because she wanted to be a composer as well, she spent even more hours learning music theory and practicing songwriting. However, Evelyn is a little different than other musicians. She is deaf. She lost most of her hearing when she was 12 years old. But that didn't stop her from becoming a musician. Evelyn knew she had a special connection to her music. She learned how to listen to music by letting sound waves travel through her body. Evelyn's music is so beautiful that she was invited to play at the opening ceremony of the 2012 Olympics. Evelyn did not let being deaf stop her from doing what she wanted to do. Even though she has a hard job, she is successful at it. She is an inspiration to musicians around the world and to all of us.

E | Answer the questions. Check your answers with a partner.

1. How old was Evelyn when she lost her hearing?

   _____

2. How did she learn to play different instruments?

   _____

3. What did she study?

   _____

4. Does Evelyn listen to music through her ears?

   _____

5. Why is Evelyn's job so challenging?

   _____

F | **Group Discussion.** Form a group with two or three other students. Discuss some of the people you learned about in this unit. What did you learn from them?

[3]A **percussionist** is a musician who plays instruments that you hit to make sound, such as drums.
[4]A **composer** is a person who writes music.

Talking about the Past

ck 2-22 **A** | Read and listen to the following article. Fill in each blank with a word from the box.

| afraid | ambition | challenges | encourages | inspire | professional |

Thirty-five-year-old Alastair Humphreys believes in challenges. For example, he faced many challenges riding his bike 46,000 miles around the world. Many thought he was a (1) _____ biker, but he wasn't! In 2011, Humphreys decided to go on small, challenging adventures inside England. He walked along Britain's infamous⁵ road, the M25. Alastair swam the Thames, slept out underneath the stars, and spent four days living off the land. Each trip he took was cold and it was challenging. To (2) _____ people, Humphreys made a video of ten (3) _____. The four-minute video (4) _____ future adventurers to sign up for a race, to do things before and after work, and to pick a place on a map and visit it. Humphreys believes you should not be (5) _____ of a challenge. He believes you should have (6) _____ too! He learned that people can be successful no matter how hard the challenges are.

B | Ask a partner questions 1–2. Your partner will give short answers using the information in the article. Then switch roles for questions 3–4.

1. Does Humphreys like challenges?
2. Name some of the challenges Humphreys faced in 2011.
3. Why did Humphreys make videos of his challenges?
4. What did Humphreys learn about people and challenges?

C | **Group Discussion.** Form a group with two or three other students. Talk about some of the challenging adventures Alastair Humphreys went though. Were the challenges difficult? Why, or why not?

D | **Self-Reflection.** Take turns asking and answering these questions with a partner.

Have you ever challenged yourself? How? Were you successful?

⁵ **Infamous** means something is well known for being bad.

ANTARCTIC CHALLENGE

Before Viewing

A | **Critical Thinking.** In Lesson **A**, you learned about different challenges. In this video, you will learn about mountain climbers who want to climb a tall rock in the challenging environment of Antarctica. Before you watch, discuss the questions below with a partner.

1. Do you think it is difficult to get to Antarctica?

2. Antarctica is a land of ice and snow. Do you think many people or animals live there?

3. Do you think it is easy to live there?

B | Read and listen to the information about Antarctica, the land of ice and snow.

track 2-23

Antarctica is large. It is larger than Europe or Australia. It covers over 5 million square miles. Its thick ice holds 70 percent of the world's fresh water. But it is also known as the world's largest desert because it gets only about two inches of snow a year. It is also the coldest place on Earth. The average temperature is -90 degrees Celsius in winter to above freezing in summer along the coast. Many tourists visit Antarctica in the summer between November and February. They go to see the beautiful frozen land, the icebergs, and animals such as whales and seals. Antarctica is also famous for its many penguins. Antarctica is a land of beauty and challenge for the people who live and work there and for the tourists who visit.

C | Use the information in exercise **B** on page 112 to help you answer the questions below. Check your answers with a partner.

1. How large is Antarctica?

   _____

2. When is summer in Antarctica?

   _____

3. What can tourists see in Antarctica?

   _____

While Viewing

A | Watch the video. Complete the sentences with the correct word.

1. The team of climbers got to Antarctica by _____.

2. They wanted to climb a very tall _____.

3. They had to walk through a lot of _____ to get to the rock.

4. The climbers did not want to _____ from the rock.

B | Watch the video again and check (✓) the different types of transportation the climbers used to get to the rock.

☐ dog sled   ☐ plane   ☐ ship   ☐ snowmobile[6]

C | Read the statements. Watch the video again. Circle **T** for *true* or **F** for *false*.

1. The rock was very dangerous to climb.   T   F

2. The mountain climbers had to be very careful
   when climbing the rock.   T   F

3. The mountain climbers had two flags.   T   F

4. The mountain climbers were not happy to
   reach the top of the rock.   T   F

After Viewing

| **Discussion.** With a partner, discuss the following questions.

1. Do you think the weather made the climb more challenging?

2. Do you think climbing the rock was risky? Explain.

3. Do you participate in risky sports? Why, or why not?

[6] A **snowmobile** is a motor vehicle used to travel in the snow.

A | Using a Dictionary. Listen and check (✓) the words you already know. Then use a dictionary to help you with any new words. These are words you will hear and use in Lesson **B**.

track 2-24

☐ activity (n.)   ☐ equipment (n.)   ☐ obstacle (n.)   ☐ sled (n.)
☐ environment (n.)   ☐ goal (n.)   ☐ realize (v.)

B | Write each word from exercise **A** next to its definition.

1. _____ anything that makes it difficult for you to do something

2. _____ to become aware of a fact or understand it

3. _____ an object that is used for traveling over snow

4. _____ surroundings in which you live or exist

5. _____ something you hope to do or achieve in the future

6. _____ something that you spend time doing

7. _____ the items you need for a particular purpose, for example, for a job or hobby

C | Listen and fill in each blank with the correct form of a word from exercise **A**. Then check your answers with a partner.

track 2-25

Dr. Michael Davis became interested in working with racehorses[7] as a young boy living outside of Houston, Texas. He (1) _____ he wanted to become a veterinarian.[8] In high school, he worked for many hours toward that (2) _____ without getting paid. Working with horses may have prepared Dr. Davis for his future job—working with (3) _____ dogs in Alaska. The sled dogs Dr. Davis works with race in the Iditarod Trail Sled Dog Race. It is a very difficult race across 1000 miles of Alaska.

Dr. Davis works in a very challenging (4) _____ and must overcome many (5) _____ such as working in extreme cold and dangerous conditions. He has to do his job as a veterinarian in a place which is very far from cities or towns that have good (6) _____. "The only thing we can count on is what we've brought with us," he says. Dr. Davis loves doing (7) _____ outside. He loves his job even though it is in a very challenging environment.

---

[7] **Racehorses** are horses that run in competitions or races.
[8] A **veterinarian** is a doctor who is trained to give medical treatment to animals.

A | **Discussion.** Look at the photos and read the captions. With a partner, discuss the challenges of working in each environment.

▲ Working on oil pipes in Alaska   ▲ An astronaut working on a space station

B | Fill in each blank with the correct form of a word from exercise **A** on page 114. Use each word only once. Then listen to the conversation and check your answers.

ck 2-26

A: Did you know that astronauts are known as space explorers? It takes them many years of hard work to reach their (1) _____ of becoming an astronaut.

B: Yeah! And they have such a cool job! Imagine working in such an extreme
(2) _____.

A: They are so brave! Last week I saw a picture of Neil Armstrong as he climbed down the ladder to step on the moon. I (3) _____ that being an astronaut is really hard and dangerous.

B: You're right. Astronauts have such a challenging job.

A: They have to be in good physical and mental shape.

B: I went to NASA last year and saw where they performed many (4) _____ under water. The underwater environment is like space.

A: Did they have a lot of special (5) _____ to work with?

B: Yes, they did! While I was at NASA, I discovered that being an astronaut is not an easy job.

A: I agree! I think a person must have a lot of ambition to become an astronaut. I think we can learn from them and not let any (6) _____ stop us from reaching our goals in life.

C | **Role-Playing.** With a partner, practice the conversation from exercise **B**. Then switch roles and practice it again.

D | **Critical Thinking.** Form a group with two or three other students. Discuss how a work environment can be challenging.

track **2-27**

Pronunciation: The Simple Past Tense -ed Endings

Regular verbs in the simple past tense that end in -ed have three different pronunciations. In Lesson **A**, we learned about the /d/ sound. In this section, we will learn about the /t/ and /id/ sounds.

-ed has a /t/ sound after these final sounds: /f/, /k/, /p/, /s/, or /sh/

Examples: *laugh* ➡ *laughed* ➡ *laugh/t/*   *ask* ➡ *asked* ➡ *ask/t/*

-ed has an /id/ sound after these final sounds: /t/ or /d/

Examples: *want* ➡ *wanted* ➡ *want/id/*   *add* ➡ *added* ➡ *add/id/*

A | Listen and repeat. Notice the different -ed endings.
track **2-28**

1. helped	2. finished	3. walked	4. looked	5. stopped
6. visited	7. repeated	8. ended	9. decided	10. needed

B | Listen and circle the ending you hear.
track **2-29**

1. (/t/) /id/   2. /t/ /id/   3. /t/ /id/   4. /t/ /id/   5. /t/ /id/

 C | Write the past tense of the verbs in the correct column. Compare your answers with a partner.

add	wish	face	like
hunt	play	listen	talk
work	inspire	enjoy	climb
~~watch~~	~~love~~	jump	~~want~~

/t/	/d/	/id/
watched	loved	wanted

Before Listening

Prior Knowledge. Look at the photos and read the captions. Then discuss the questions with a partner.

▲ A New York taxi   ▲ A chef preparing food

1. Did you ever ride in a taxi? Where did you go?
2. Do you think taxi drivers have a difficult job? Why, or why not?
3. Did you ever eat in a restaurant?
4. Who cooks the food in a restaurant?
5. Do you think chefs have a challenging job? Why, or why not?

Listening: A Conversation

A | **Listening for the Main Idea.** Listen to the conversation. Circle the main idea.

ack 2-30

The speakers are talking about _____.

a. how hard it is to find work
b. the challenges of their work
c. learning new skills for their work

B | **Listening for Details.** Listen again. Write short answers to the questions.

ack 2-30

1. What jobs do the speakers have?

   One is a _____ and the other is a _____.

2. Where do they live?

   They live in _____.

3. Name two challenges the taxi driver faced at work.

   a. She worked _____ hours a day.

   b. The customers were not always _____.

4. Name two challenges the chef faced at work.

   a. He _____ long hours in a hot kitchen.

   b. _____ expected the best food every time.

After Listening

Self-Reflection. Discuss with a partner which job you think is better: a taxi driver or a chef.

track 2-31

A | Making Inferences. Listen to and read the following sentences. Then circle the correct inference.

1. It takes many years of practice and dedication to learn to play the piano.

   a. It is easy to learn to play the piano.

   b. Some people never learn to play the piano.

   c. You can learn to play the piano if you work hard at it.

2. If you work on oil pipes in Alaska, you often have to work outside in snow and very cold weather.

   a. Oil pipe workers in Alaska have to work in a challenging environment.

   b. Working in Alaska is interesting.

   c. Oil pipe workers in Alaska have an easy job.

3. Olympic athletes start practicing at a young age and work for many hours every day, for many years.

   a. It does not take a lot of work to become an Olympic athlete.

   b. It takes a lot of time and work to become an Olympic athlete.

   c. If you start practicing at a young age, you will become an Olympic athlete.

Critical Thinking Focus

Making Inferences

To make an inference means to guess what is being said without the person saying it directly.

For example, if a person tells you to take an umbrella with you, a logical inference is that it is going to rain.

track 2-32

B | Listen to the conversation. Circle the correct answers.

1. The article Melissa and her friend read was about two _____.
   a. businessmen   b. businesswomen   c. businesses

2. The women believed in _____.
   a. their friends   b. their family   c. themselves

3. Without persistence, the women would never have become _____ businesswomen.
   a. successful   b. happy   c. interesting

4. We can infer that most successful businesspeople _____ in themselves.
   a. don't believe   b. believe   c. never believe

C | Discussion. With a partner, discuss the questions below.

1. Is it harder for women to be successful in business? Explain.

2. Do you agree that taking risks is necessary to be successful?

Grammar: The Simple Past Tense

We use the simple past tense to talk about:

- a completed action in the past—the action started and finished at a time in the past.

  Example: *Evelyn **became** a famous musician even though she was deaf.*

- a series of completed actions.

  Example: *Erik Weihenmayer **learned** how to ski, mountain bike, and climb mountains.*

- duration in the past—used with expressions such as *for one day*, *for five minutes*, *for two months*, etc.

  Example: *Dr. Davis **had** a challenging job in Alaska **for two years**.*

A | Complete each sentence with either the simple present tense or the simple past tense of the verb in parentheses. Then listen to the sentences and check your answers.

track 2-33

1. Walt Disney was unsuccessful in many businesses before he _____ (start) Disneyland.

2. The ice and cold in Alaska _____ (make) it a difficult environment to work in.

3. Humphreys _____ (walk) along the M25.

4. Astronauts _____ (practice) how to work underwater before they go into space.

5. Working as a chef _____ (be) challenging because you work in hot kitchens for many hours.

B | Circle the correct answer. Then check your answers with a partner.

1. Musicians _____ many hours every day.

   a. practice   b. practiced

2. A few years ago, Erik Weihenmayer and Chad Jukes _____ one of the most challenging mountains.

   a. climb   b. climbed

3. Today, oil pipe workers _____ in challenging environments.

   a. work   b. worked

4. Neil Armstrong _____ the first man to step on the moon.

   a. is   b. was

C | **Critical Thinking.** With your partner, discuss the questions.

Which one of these people has the most challenging job? Why?

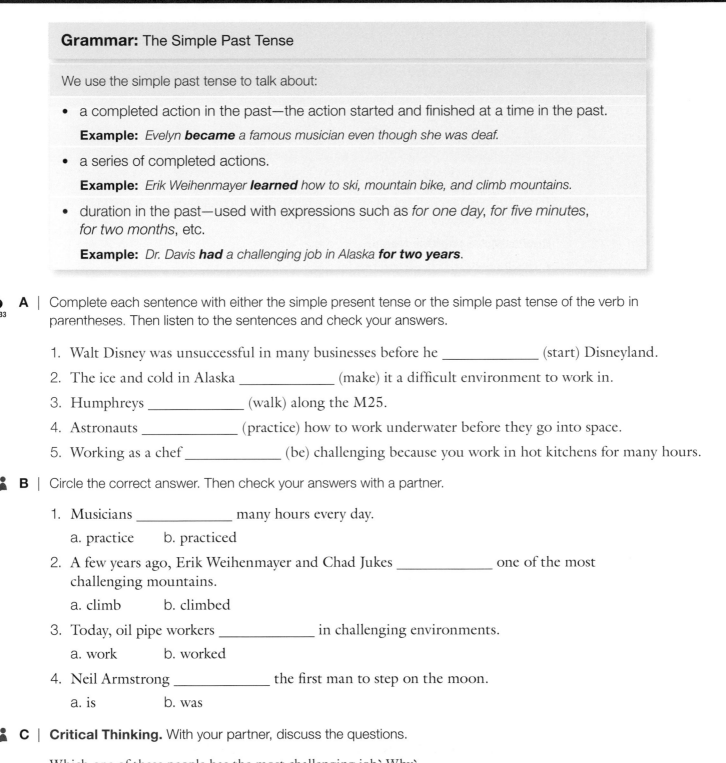

▲ veterinarian   ▲ marine biologist   ▲ pilot

In this section, you are going to give a presentation about a challenge you faced. The challenge can be in school, sports, or at work. You will make notes to help you present.

Presentation Skills: Presenting to a Group Using Notes

When presenting, it is helpful to have notes to guide you during your presentation. It is important to remember that these notes are *not* for you to read from. They are to remind you what you want to say.

How to Make and Use Notes:

- Use 3x5 or 4x6 index cards.
- Number your index cards.
- Write the main ideas of your presentation, important facts, numbers, dates, etc.
- Write key phrases, not complete sentences.
- When presenting, look at your notes, but don't read them.
- Before you present, practice, practice, and practice again using your notes.

A | Self-Reflection. Put a check (✓) next to the topic you would like to present.

☐ An academic challenge—Did you study a subject or language that was difficult to learn?

☐ A sports challenge—Did you play a sport such as football, swimming, etc., that was difficult to learn?

☐ A work challenge—Did you need to have skills for a job that were difficult to learn?

B | Organizing Ideas. Fill in the blanks to help organize your presentation.

Topic: _____

What was the challenge? _____

What did you do to overcome the challenge? _____

Were you successful? _____

C | Making Notes. On three or four index cards, write the main ideas of your presentation.

D | Presentation. Present your topic to a small group of students. Remember you can look at your notes but don't read them.

Lost and Found

ACADEMIC PATHWAYS
Lesson A: Listening to a Guided Tour
            Talking about the Past
Lesson B: Listening to a Conversation
            Role-Playing

Think and Discuss

1. Look at the photo. What do you see?
2. How old do you think the mask is? Why?
3. What do you think this unit will be about?

The mask of ▶
the Egyptian King
Tutankhamun

Exploring the Theme: Lost and Found

Look at the photos and read the information. Then discuss the questions.

1. Why is it important to study groups of people from the past?

2. What can we learn from things people made very long ago?

3. Which time in the past do you want to visit? Why?

▼ Archaeological dig site in Egypt

Mesopotamian Civilization,
the Akkadian Dynasty, 2350–2150 BC

Iraq

A life-size bronze head found near Nineveh (near Baghdad, Iraq)

Ancient Egyptian Civilization,
the New Kingdom Period, 1539–1075 BC

Egypt

An ancient Egyptian ship moving a body

PAST

Ancient Chinese Civilization,

2100–256 BC

China

An ancient Chinese bronze horse-drawn cart and horse with rider

Maya Civilization,

the Classic Period,
AD 250–900

Honduras
Belize
Mexico
Guatemala
El Salvador

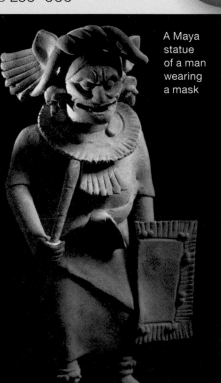

A Maya statue of a man wearing a mask

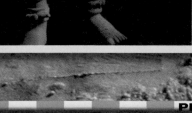

BC AD

PRESENT

A | Using a Dictionary. Listen and check (✓) the words you already know. Use a dictionary to help you with any new words. These are words you will hear and use in Lesson **A**.

track 2-34

- ☐ capital (n.)
- ☐ civilization (n.)
- ☐ internal (adj.)
- ☐ temple (n.)
- ☐ century (n.)
- ☐ emperor (n.)
- ☐ resources (n.)
- ☐ valuable (adj.)

B | Match each word with its definition.

1. emperor _____   a. a group of people with its own rules and culture
2. capital _____   b. a man who rules a country or place
3. civilization _____   c. a word used to describe things that happen inside a country
4. internal _____   d. the city where a country's government meets

C | Meaning from Context. Read and listen to the article about a lost civilization. Notice the words in **blue**. Then write a word next to its definition below.

track 2-35

What Happened to ANGKOR WAT?

The kingdom of Angkor Wat was in Cambodia. It lasted from the 9th to the 15th **century**. 750,000 people lived in its **capital**, Angkor. It was the largest city of its time. Angkor was known as a royal city. The kings of Angkor said they were world **emperors** of Hindu teachings. They built **temples** for themselves. People did not use money in Angkor. They used rice instead. Over centuries, the people of Angkor built hundreds of miles of waterways. The **civilization** learned how to save and use water. Other kingdoms had problems with too little or too much water.

This made Angkor's waterways very **valuable resources**. But over time, the world around Angkor changed. Angkor faced economic and religious challenges. Also, the weather changed. Finally, Angkor's water system, which had worked for 600 years, broke down. This caused **internal** fighting and the end of an amazing civilization.

1. _____ things that a country has and can use to increase its wealth
2. _____ buildings used for the worship of a god or gods
3. _____ 100 years
4. _____ very useful or worth a lot

A | Complete the conversation with the correct form of a word from exercise **A** on page 124.

A: Do you know where Angkor Wat is?

B: Yes. Angkor Wat is in Cambodia.

A: How long did the kingdom last?

B: It lasted from the 9th to the 15th (1) _____.

A: Wow! That's almost 600 years! How many people lived in its (2) _____, Angkor?

B: I think almost 750,000 people lived there.

A. I think it's interesting that the kings called themselves world (3) _____.

B: They also had many (4) _____ made to themselves.

A: Yes, you are right. Something else that is interesting is that they had no money!

B: Right! They used rice instead of money. But what is Angkor famous for?

A: Angkor is famous for its old waterways. They were a very (5) _____ resource.

B: What finally happened to Angkor?

A: (6) _____ fighting ended that amazing civilization.

B | Listen to the conversation and check your answers. Then practice the conversation with a partner.

track 2-36

C | **Discussion.** With your partner, discuss the questions below.

1. What is the capital of your country?

2. Does your country have an emperor? What country does?

3. What valuable resources does your country have?

4. Does your city have temples? Can you name countries that have temples?

A moat surrounding Angkor ▶

Before Listening

 Prior Knowledge. In a small group, discuss the questions below.

1. What is in a museum?
2. Where is the British Museum?
3. What is in the photo?
4. Do you think the Cyrus Cylinder is important? Why?

▲ The Cyrus Cylinder in the British Museum

Listening: A Guided Tour

🎧 track 2-37

A | Listening for Main Ideas. Read the statements and answer choices. Then listen and choose the best answer to complete each statement.

1. Cyrus the Great established the first _____.
   a. Roman Empire
   b. Persian Empire
   c. Mongolian Empire

2. The Cyrus Cylinder is important because it has _____ written on it.
   a. laws
   b. numbers
   c. dates

3. The laws protected people of different religions and _____.
   a. ages
   b. professions
   c. cultures

▲ Persepolis: Persian nobles

🎧 track 2-37

B | Listening for Details. Listen again. Choose the best answer to complete each statement.

1. The Great Court has information desks, restaurants, and a big _____.
   a. tea room   b. reading room   c. library

2. Information about ancient Persia is in room _____.
   a. 15   b. 50   c. 52

3. Iran's civilization is over _____ years old.
   a. 2500   b. 250   c. 2550

4. The Cyrus Cylinder was discovered in _____.
   a. 8097   b. 1879   c. 1897

After Listening

A | **Self-Reflection.** Form a group with two or three other students. Discuss the questions below.

1. Do you like museums? Why, or why not?

2. When you go, do you take a guided tour?

B | **Critical Thinking.** Discuss the question with your group.

Why was the Cyrus Cylinder an important discovery?

Pronunciation: Word Stress

track 2-38

In English, when we say a word, the first syllable is usually louder than the other syllables. This is called *word stress*. Word stress is a very important part of spoken English. There are three rules about word stress:

1. Every word has just one stressed syllable.

2. Most two-syllable *nouns* and *adjectives* are stressed on the **first** syllable.

   Examples: **A**pril, **an**cient, **ta**ble, **mo**ther, **hap**py, **yel**low, **ho**tel

3. Many two-syllable *verbs* are stressed on the **second** syllable.

   Examples: de**cide**, re**peat**, be**gin**

track 2-39

A | Listen to the following words. <u>Underline</u> the stressed syllable.

1. <u>tem</u>ple   2. paper   3. answer   4. people   5. prevent

6. survive   7. quiet   8. explain   9. sleepy   10. perfect

B | With a partner, practice saying the words in exercise **A**.

Grammar: Informational Past Tense Questions

We ask questions to get information or to clarify information we have. Here are two ways we ask past tense questions.

Informational Past Tense Questions: *To Be*

Verb (past tense form of *to be*) + subject
    Rania was at the Science Museum yesterday. ➡ ***Was** Rania at the Science Museum yesterday?*
    The children were in the temple. ➡ ***Were** the children in the temple?*

Informational Past Tense Questions: *Yes/No* Questions

Did + subject + basic verb form
    Rania saw interesting things at the museum. ➡ ***Did** Rania **see** interesting things at the museum?*
    You had a tour guide. ➡ ***Did** you **have** a tour guide?*

A | Read the conversation below. Choose the correct word to complete the sentences. Then compare your answers with a partner and practice the conversation.

A: (1) _____ (**Was / Were**) you in Egypt when they discovered the 4300-year-old pyramid of Queen Sesheshet?

B: Yes, I was. It was a very important discovery.

A: (2) _____ (**Was / Were**) archaeologists surprised to find the pyramid?

B: Yes. They thought there were no more pyramids in the area.

A: What is so important about the pyramid of Queen Sesheshet?

B: Her pyramid was built by her son, Teti.

A: Did pharaohs often (3) _____ (**build / built**) pyramids for their mothers?

B: Yes, they did. Mothers in ancient Egypt were loved very much.

A: (4) _____ (**Was / Were**) this their way of thanking their mothers?

B: Yes, it was. Also, Queen Sesheshet came from a very powerful family.

A: Hmm. I guess that is why the pyramid was so big. (5) _____ (**Was / Were**) archaeologists very excited about the discovery?

B: Yes, they were. To discover a queen's pyramid is a very special occasion.

▲ The site of Queen Sesheshet's pyramid

B | Write the correct verb form in the blanks. Take turns asking the questions with your partner.

1. _____Did_____ (do) you _____see_____ (see) your friend yesterday?

2. _____ (do) the boy _____ (visit) Pompeii last summer?

3. _____ (do) Claire _____ (take) pictures of the Cyrus Cylinder last month?

4. _____ (do) the family _____ (think) Angkor Wat was interesting?

Language Function: Expressing Past Facts and Generalizations with *Used To*

We use *used to* to talk about past facts that are no longer true.
Subject + *used to* + basic verb form
Example: *The pharaohs **used to build** pyramids for their mothers.*

Here is how we form a question about past facts that are no longer true.
Did + subject + *use to* + basic verb form
Example: ***Did** pharaohs **use to build** pyramids for their mothers?*

A | Complete each sentence using *used to* and the correct form of the verbs in parentheses.

1. In ancient Peru, surgeons _____ (treat) head injuries.

2. In ancient Mexico and Egypt, they _____ (build) pyramids.

3. In ancient Rome, only boys _____ (have) higher education.

4. In ancient China, men _____ (rule) the family.

B | Work with a partner. Look at the illustration and answer the questions.

1. Did people in ancient Greece use to build walls around the cities?

2. Did men use to wear short dresses?

3. Did women use to wear long, colorful dresses?

4. Did people in ancient Greece use to travel on horses?

▲ A drawing of palace life in ancient Greece

C | Complete the sentences with your partner.

1. People in ancient Egypt used to build pyramids, _____

2. In ancient Rome, only boys used to have higher education, _____

3. Angkor used to be the capital of Angkor Wat, _____

4. The Cyrus Cylinder used to protect people of different religions and cultures, _____

a. before the end of the civilization.

b. but today it is in the British Museum.

c. but today girls in Rome have higher education, too.

d. but now they build tall buildings.

D | **Making Inferences.** Form a group with two or three other students. Discuss the questions.

1. Why did people use to build walls around their cities?

2. Why did men use to wear short dresses in Greece?

track **2-40**

E | Read and listen to the article. <u>Underline</u> *used to*.

Were Aztec, Olmec, and Maya Rubber-Making Masters?

Three thousand years ago, ancient civilizations in Mexico and Central America used to make rubber. The Aztec, Olmec, and Maya civilizations used to make rubber from trees and plants. Some of the rubber they made used to bounce.[1] The Mayas used to play a lot of ball games. They made balls for their games with this rubber. In ancient Maya, games used to play an important part in their religion. These ball games were played to show good against evil.[2] Sometimes the games ended in human sacrifice.[3] The losers were beheaded—that means they used to have their heads cut off!

F | Ask a partner questions 1–3. Your partner will give short answers using the information in the article in exercise **E**. Then switch roles for questions 4–6.

1. What did ancient civilizations in Mexico and Central America use to make?
2. What did they use to make rubber from?
3. Did the rubber use to bounce?
4. Did the Mayas use to play games?
5. Why did they use to play ball games?
6. What used to happen to the losers of the ball games?

G | **Critical Thinking.** Form a group with two or three other students. Look at the photo in exercise **E**. Discuss the questions below.

1. How many different ball games can you think of?
2. What do you think the hoop[4] in the photo was used for?
3. What kind of ball games do you think the Mayas used to play?

> Did you know that in parts of Mexico, a ball game named *ulama* is still played? *Ulama* is very similar to the ancient ball games of the Aztecs or Mayas. The big difference is that the losing team does not lose their heads!

[1] To **bounce** means to go up and down.
[2] **Evil** means morally very bad.
[3] A **sacrifice** is a person or animal that is killed to thank or please a god.
[4] A **hoop** is a ring.

Talking about the Past

A | Look at the time line. It shows when some ancient civilizations began. Answer yes or no to the questions below. Then ask a partner the questions. Your partner answers, then corrects the statements.

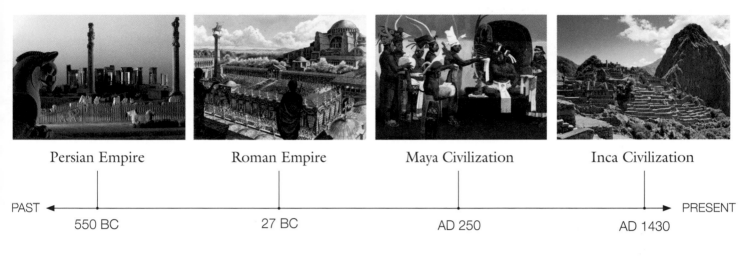

| Persian Empire | Roman Empire | Maya Civilization | Inca Civilization |

PAST ← 550 BC — 27 BC — AD 250 — AD 1430 → PRESENT

1. Did the Maya civilization come before the Roman Empire? _____
2. Did the Persian Empire come after the Inca civilization? _____
3. Did the Roman Empire come before the Inca civilization? _____
4. Did the Inca civilization come after the Maya Civilization? _____

B | Read the passage. Then discuss the questions below with a partner.

Six Characteristics⁵ of Ancient Civilizations

All civilizations have special characteristics. In ancient civilizations, people lived in big areas. They made large monuments such as pyramids and temples. These monuments often had unique⁶ art on the walls. Also, every civilization had a written language. They had a system for controlling people and land. People of ancient civilizations did different types of work such as farming, selling goods, trading, etc. Finally, in ancient civilizations people were separated into social classes.

1. How many characteristics did ancient civilizations have? Name three of them.
2. Another word for a pyramid or temple is a _____.
3. What did monuments often have on them?

C | **Self-Reflection.** Form a group with two or three other students. Discuss the question below.

What is important in a civilization? Explain.

⁵ **Characteristics** are qualities or features.
⁶ **Unique** means special, different, or one of a kind.

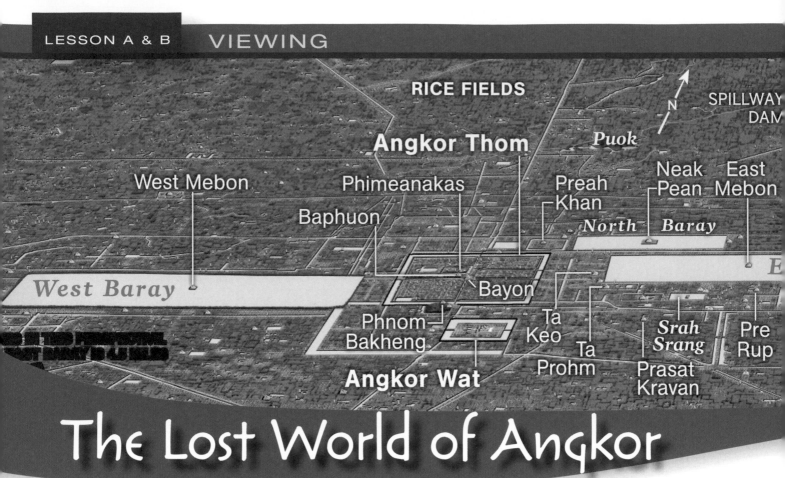

RICE FIELDS

Angkor Thom

Puok

N

SPILLWAY
DAM

West Mebon

Phimeanakas

Preah
Khan

Neak   East
Pean Mebon

North *Baray*

Baphuon

West Baray

Bayon

E

Phnom
Bakheng

Ta
Keo

*Srah
Srang*

Pre
Rup

Ta
Prohm

Angkor Wat

Prasat
Kravan

The Lost World of Angkor

Before Viewing

A | **Understanding Visuals.** Work with a partner. Look at the map of Imperial Angkor. Discuss the following questions.

1. What important food source was Angkor surrounded by?

2. Did Angkor have a lot of water systems? Where are they?

B | **Prior Knowledge.** In Lesson **A** of this unit, you learned about the kingdom of Angkor Wat. This video is about the ancient city of Angkor. Discuss the questions with your partner.

1. Where is Angkor Wat?

2. What is Angkor Wat famous for?

C | **Using a Dictionary.** Match each word to its definition. Use a dictionary to help you.

1. fail (v.) _____   a. to make something by cutting and shaping

2. jungle (n.) _____   b. to not work

3. carve (v.) _____   c. a rock

4. stone (n.) _____   d. a forest with many trees and plants

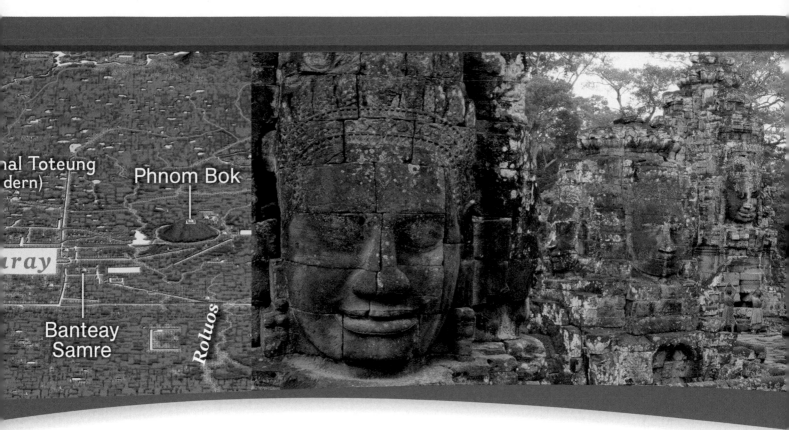

While Viewing

🖥 **A | Viewing for Numbers.** Read the sentences below. Then watch the video. Complete the sentences with the correct numbers.

1. _____*500*_____ years ago Angkor covered more than _____ square kilometers.

2. In _____ a French explorer found the city.

3. The temple of Bayan has more than _____ faces carved in stone.

4. In the _____ century, people attacked and burned Angkor Wat.

🖥 **B |** Read the sentences below. Then watch the video again. Write **T** for *true* or **F** for *false*.

1. The Khmer Empire ruled much of northeast Asia. _____

2. During the 13th century, about 750,000 people lived there. _____

3. The temple of Angkor Wat was built during the mid-1100s. _____

4. In the 12th century, people attacked and burned the city. _____

After Viewing

👥 **A | Critical Thinking.** Form a group with two or three other students. Discuss the questions.

1. In the video, you heard that Angkor had an amazing water system. Why do you think the water system was so important for the people of Angkor?

2. How important is water for a city? What might happen to a city if there is not enough water?

👥 **B | Discussion.** With a partner, look at the photo and discuss what you think the Buddhist monks are doing.

A | Using a Dictionary. Listen and check (✓) the words you already know. Then use a dictionary to help you with any new words. These are words you will hear and use in Lesson **B**.

☐ artifact (n.) ☐ estimate (v.) ☐ gold (n.) ☐ site (n.)
☐ chief (n.) ☐ excavate (v.) ☐ native (adj.) ☐ treasure (n.)

B | Write each word from exercise **A** next to its definition.

1. _____ born in a place or belonging to a particular place

2. _____ an object made by humans found at an archaeological dig

3. _____ the head or leader of a group of people

4. _____ jewels, money, and other things of value

5. _____ to dig or make a hole in the ground

6. _____ a place or location

7. _____ a precious yellow metal, often used in jewelry

8. _____ to guess the value or amount of something

C | Meaning from Context. Read and listen to the article. Notice the words in **blue**.

The GOLDEN CHIEFS of Panama

In 2005, archaeologist Julia Mayo and her team began to **excavate** a cemetery[7] in Panama. The cemetery was more than 1000 years old. Many **treasures** were found at this **site**. In 2010, she and her team uncovered a powerful warrior **chief** wearing **gold**. In 2011, they uncovered another chief. Specialists at the Smithsonian Institution[8] studied what Mayo's team found. They learned something important about this ancient civilization. The **native** people lived in simple houses, but they were rich and cultured enough to understand fine art.

Mayo thinks the cemetery has about 20 more chiefs like the two she excavated. Because her team of 10 works slowly, in four years they have dug up just two percent of the cemetery. She **estimates** that if work continues at this speed, the last **artifact** will be excavated 196 years from now!

[7] A **cemetery** is a place where dead people are buried.
[8] The **Smithsonian Institution** is a U.S. research and educational organization.

A | Fill in each blank with the correct form of a word from exercise **A** on page 134.

1. Julia Mayo found many treasures at the archaeological _____.

2. Her team was excited when they found _____ in the ground.

3. Not long after they started to dig, they found a powerful _____.

4. The warrior chiefs were covered in _____ when they were buried.

5. The houses of the _____ people were simple.

6. Mayo and her team have much more of the cemetery to _____.

7. She _____ that it will take 196 years to find all of the artifacts in the cemetery.

B | **Discussion.** Look at the photo. With a partner, discuss the following questions.

1. What are these people doing?

2. Do you think they work slowly or quickly? Why?

3. Why do you think they have buckets?[9]

4. Do you think there are more artifacts at this site? Why, or why not?

C | **Self-Reflection.** With your partner, discuss the questions below.

1. Do you think working as an archaeologist is an interesting job? Explain.

2. What things are interesting about working on an archaeological site?

3. What things are not interesting about working on an archaeological site?

[9] **Buckets** are round, open containers with handles.

track **2-43**

Listening for Emphasized Words

When listening to a conversation or lecture, pay attention to the loudest and slowest words. These emphasized words usually contain important information. Less important words are usually spoken quickly and softly. In a question such as, "Did you *find anything*?," the words *find* and *anything* are stressed or emphasized. In the sentence, "Not long after they started to dig, they found a *warrior* made of *gold*," the words *warrior* and *gold* are emphasized.

Before Listening

track **2-44**

A | Listen to a commercial for archaeological tours. Circle the word or words that are emphasized in each sentence.

1. Tired of staying home?

   (a. tired)   b. staying   c. home

2. Need a vacation?

   a. need   b. a   c. vacation

3. Give us a call!

   a. give   b. us   c. call

4. We specialize in archaeological tours.

   a. we   b. specialize   c. archaeological

5. For more information, call 1-800-555-1800.

   a. more   b. information   c. 1-800-555-1800

B | **Predicting Content.** You will hear two people talk about looking for lost treasure. With a partner, decide which topic they will probably NOT talk about. Check (✓) your answer.

☐ Finding lost treasure is exciting.   ☐ You always find treasure when you look for it.

☐ Workers find an ancient archaeological site.

Listening: A Conversation

track **2-45**

A | **Listening for Details.** Listen to the conversation. Then choose the correct answer to complete each statement.

1. Her house used to have _____.

   a. a small yard   b. no yard   c. a big yard

2. Her sister put her hand in a _____.

   a. small hole in a tree   b. big hole in a tree   c. small hole in the wall

3. There was a _____ in the tree.

   a. big box   b. shoe   c. small box

B | Note-Taking. Listen to the conversation again. Complete the sentences.

A: When you were younger, did you ever look for lost (1) _____ in your backyard?

B: Yeah, I did! I remember when we had just moved into a house with a big backyard. My sister and I went into the backyard and started exploring it. We thought we might find lost (2) _____ there.

A: Did you find anything?

B: Yes, as a matter of fact, we did! One of the trees had a small hole in it. The hole was just big enough for my sister to put her hand in. She pulled out a very small box! Inside the box was a ring. I don't think the ring was very valuable. We never had anyone (3) _____ its value.

A: Well, I never found any lost treasures. But I read that some workers in Scotland uncovered some (4) _____. They found (5) _____ Roman shoes. The shoes were over (6) _____ years old!

B: Really! How did they find them?

A: Well, workers were digging to build a supermarket. They uncovered very old shoes. But that's not all! They started to (7) _____ some more. They found Roman jewelry, coins, and pottery at the site.

B: Wow! Imagine that. The workers were responsible for uncovering a very wealthy archaeological (8) _____. Now that's what you call finding a lost treasure!

C | Checking Predictions. Look back at the prediction you made in exercise **B** on page 136. Then listen to the conversation again. Was your prediction correct?

After Listening

Critical Thinking. Form a group with two or three other students. Discuss the question.

You are in a public park. Your dog digs up a treasure. What do you do with it?

An archaeological site in Scotland with Roman artifacts ▶

Grammar: The Conjunction *Because*

Because is a conjunction or a connecting word. We use *because* when giving the reason for something.

Examples: *I went to the museum* **because** ➡ *I wanted to see the artifacts.*
Archaeologists learned about Peru's surgeons **because** ➡ *they found the skulls.*

🎧
track **2-46**

A | **Using a Dictionary.** Read and listen to the article. Use a dictionary to help you with any new words.

Inca Skull Surgeons Were "Highly Skilled"

In Peru, on a site near the ancient Inca capital of Cuzco, archaeologists found very old skulls. These skulls belonged to natives and were more than 2000 years old. For the archaeologists, these skulls were more valuable than treasures of gold. The skulls showed that Inca surgeons made holes in patients' skulls to treat head injuries. The procedure was usually performed on injured men. These men probably got injured while fighting. In the beginning, the procedure was new. People who had the surgery died. But by the 1400s, Inca surgeons had more experience with the procedure. Archaeologists estimate almost 90 percent survived the surgery. Today, surgeons perform similar procedures on people who have severe head trauma.

B | Complete the sentences. Then check your answers with a partner.

1. The skulls were valuable to archaeologists because

     they showed how Inca surgeons used to treat head injuries.

2. The Inca surgeons made holes in patients' heads because

     _____

3. In the beginning, many injured men died because

     _____

C | With your partner, take turns asking and answering the questions.

1. Why did the men probably need head surgery?

2. Why do you think almost 90 percent of the men survived the procedure by the 1400s?

3. Why do surgeons perform similar procedures today?

D | Read and listen to the conversation. <u>Underline</u> the clarification expressions you hear.

A: Last summer we went to Turkey. We visited an ancient Roman spa city!

B: I'm sorry, could you repeat what you just said? A spa city? What is that?

A: Let me explain. In 1998, archaeologists discovered the ancient spa city of Allianoi.

B: What do you mean? Why did you call it a spa city?

A: Because the city was famous for its bathhouses.[10] Important Romans would visit the city to go to the bathhouses. That is why it is called *The Spa City*.

B: Wow! Are the bathhouses still there?

A: Yes and no.

B: What do you mean by yes and no?

A: Well, they are building a dam[11] near Allianoi. So, to save the bathhouses, Turkish officials decided to rebury the site with sand! They want to save the bathhouses by keeping them buried under sand.

▲ A bathhouse in Turkey

E | **Role-Playing.** Take turns reading the conversation in exercise **D** with a partner.

F | **Note-Taking.** Close your book and listen to the conversation in exercise **D** again. Take notes on what you hear.

G | **Discussion.** Form a group with two or three other students. Discuss what you recall about Allianoi. Use your notes to help you recall facts.

ck 2-47

k 2-47

> **Student to Student**
>
> **Asking for Clarification**
>
> Sometimes you do not understand something you hear. Here are some expressions you can use to ask for clarification. These expressions let people know you did not understand what was said.
> *I'm sorry, I didn't understand what you said about …*
> *I'm sorry, could you repeat what you just said?*
> *What do you mean?*
> *Could you explain it one more time?*

> **Critical Thinking Focus**
>
> **Recalling Facts**
>
> Recalling information is an important skill. Take notes during class. Then look at your notes when you go home or before your next class.

---

[10] **Bathhouses** are buildings that have baths inside them.
[11] A **dam** is a wall built to control water.

In this section, you are going to practice role-playing. Role-playing is an important part of learning language. It involves different language functions such as asking for clarification, asking for directions, giving directions, etc. In role-playing, you need to use the right language to express those functions.

A | Read the following conversation. This is an example of what you will do in exercise **B**.

A: Last year, when you had free time, where did you go?

B: I went to <u>museums</u>.

A: Which one did you go to?

B: I went to <u>the Houston Museum of Natural Science</u>.

A: I'm sorry, what did you say?

B: I said I went to <u>the Houston Museum of Natural Science</u>.

A: What did you like about <u>the Houston Museum of Natural Science</u>?

B: Well, I liked <u>everything. But I really liked the new Terra Cotta Warriors Exhibit</u>.

A: Do you recommend it?

B: Absolutely!

▲ A terra cotta warrior

Presentation Skills: Using Body Language

When we speak and listen, we use body language. Body language communicates meaning and emotions and helps keep interest. Body language includes the following: eye contact, facial expressions, posture, and movements. For example, try to look at the person you are speaking to more than half the time. Or, nod your head once in a while to let the speaker know you are listening and you understand.

B | **Creating a Dialog.** Complete the sentences to make a conversation.

A: Last year, when you had free time, where did you go?

B: I went to _____.

A: I'm sorry, could you repeat what you just said?

B: I said I went to _____.

A: Which one did you go to?

B: I went to _____.

A: What did you like about _____?

B: I liked _____.

A: Do you recommend it?

B: Absolutely!

C | **Role-Playing.** Take turns reading dialogs with a partner. Remember to use body language.

A New View

ACADEMIC PATHWAYS
Lesson A: Listening to a Scientific Talk
Conducting a Survey
Lesson B: Listening to a Debate between Friends
Participating in a Debate

Think and Discuss

1. Look at the photo. What do you see?
2. How do you think technology might help us in the future?
3. What do you think this unit will be about?

A bionic body ▶

The
Future
is **Here**

Cutting-edge bionic arm

Exploring the Theme:
A New View

Look at the photos and read the captions and the information. Then discuss the questions.

1. Do you think people will want cars that fly? Why, or why not?

2. Do you want to live underwater? Why, or why not?

3. Do you think it is a good idea to grow vegetables and fruit in our apartments? Explain.

Welcome to the future! Here is a quick look at what the near future might be like for you. People will fly their cars to work or school. Some cities may be underwater. You might live in an apartment where you can grow vegetables and fruit. Or, you might have robots that will deliver your mail, help you clean your house, and even talk to you! The big question is, are you ready for the future?

▼ A flying car

▼ A city underwater

▼ A garden project

A | **Meaning from Context.** Look at the photos and read the captions. Then read and listen to the sentences below. Notice the words in **blue**. These are words you will hear and use in Lesson **A**.

track 2-48

1. A device can help some people live an easier life.

2. Robots with artificial intelligence can do many things.

3. Robots can respond to a command given to them.

4. Our brains control how we think and what we do.

5. Our brains communicate to the rest of our body.

6. The brain sends a signal to artificial limbs telling them to move.

7. People without a limb often have difficulties doing everyday activities.

8. Bionic limbs or parts will allow people to live normal lives.

▲ Aiden Kenny has devices implanted in his ears so he can hear.

B | Write each word in **blue** from exercise **A** next to its definition. Use a dictionary to help you.

1. _____ (n.) an instruction, an order

2. _____ (n.) a tool or machine used to perform a job or function

3. _____ (n.) an action that sends a message, often without words

4. _____ (adj.) using a mechanical or electrical machine to improve body functions

5. _____ (n.) a body part; for example, a leg, arm, etc.

6. _____ (adj.) something made by humans

7. _____ (v.) to manage or have power over

8. _____ (v.) to exchange information

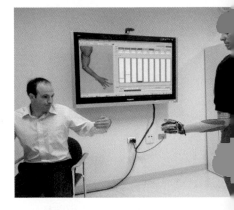

▲ Amanda Kitts imagines a hand movement and moves her bionic arm.

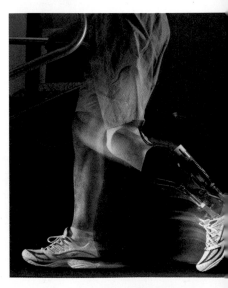

▲ A person runs on a treadmill with a bionic leg.

A | Fill in each blank with the correct form of a word in **blue** from exercise **A** on page 144. Use each word only once.

BIONICS

In 2006, Amanda Kitts was in a car accident. She lost her left arm. Amanda volunteered to test an (1) _____ arm. So, doctors put a (2) _____ in her nervous system. This device replies to (3) _____ from the brain. Amanda's brain (4) _____ the artificial (5) _____.
It is called a "bionic arm."

Today doctors are implanting devices such as cameras, microphones, and motors in patients. As a result, the blind can see, the deaf can hear, and Amanda Kitts can pick up a cup of coffee with her (6) _____ arm. Jo Ann Lewis, a blind woman, is another person being helped by the science of the future. She can now see the shapes of trees with the help of a tiny[1] camera. The camera (7) _____ with the nerve in her eye. And Aiden, who was born deaf, can hear. A microphone picks up and sends (8) _____ to his ear. Of course, not everything will work perfectly. But patients with bionic parts are given tools that will help them live more normal lives.

B | Complete each sentence with the correct form of a word from exercise **A** on page 144. Then discuss your ideas with a partner.

1. In the future, some people will have _____ body parts.

2. Artificial _____ will do everything a real arm or leg can do.

3. A _____ placed in Jo Ann Lewis's eye lets her see the shapes of trees.

4. The brain sends _____ to our hand when we want to pick up a cup.

C | **Self-Reflection.** With your partner, discuss the question below.

Which do you think is more difficult to use—a bionic arm or a bionic leg? Why?

[1] **Tiny** means very small.

Pronunciation: Contractions with *Will*

We often use *will* when we talk about the future. In spoken English, *will* is often contracted or made shorter. *Will* becomes *'ll* and is joined to the subject.

I
You
He
She   } *'ll*
It
We
They

Examples: *I will see you tomorrow.*   ➡   ***I'll** see you tomorrow.*
He will give a lecture.   ➡   ***He'll** give a lecture.*
We will buy a robot.   ➡   ***We'll** buy a robot.*

A | Work with a partner. Practice reading each pair of sentences.

1. He will give a talk on cloning.   ➡   He'll give a talk on cloning.
2. They will ask about cloning people.   ➡   They'll ask about cloning people.
3. We will go to the museum.   ➡   We'll go to the museum.
4. You will like the book on cloning.   ➡   You'll like the book on cloning.

B | Rewrite the sentences using contractions. Read your new sentences to your partner.

1. They will watch a movie about robots.

_____

2. He will get a bionic arm.

_____

3. She will clone her pet when it dies.

_____

Before Listening

 Prior Knowledge. You are going to listen to a talk by a science professor. But first, discuss the following questions with a partner.

1. Do you know what a dinosaur is?
2. Do you know what happened to them?
3. Do you think it is possible for scientists to make copies of dinosaurs?

Listening: A Scientific Talk

🎧 **A | Listening for the Main Idea.** Read the sentences. Then listen to the talk and circle the main idea.

ack 2-50

a. The professor is giving a talk on movies.

b. The professor is giving a talk on cloning.

c. The professor is giving a talk on dinosaurs.

🎧 **B | Listening for Details.** Read the sentences and answer choices below. Then listen again and choose the correct answers.

ack 2-50

1. The professor mentions the movie _____.

   a. *Star Wars*

   b. *E.T.*

   c. *Jurassic Park*

2. The professor gives an example of how we can now clone _____.

   a. dogs

   b. mice

   c. cats

3. The last Ice Age was about _____ years ago.

   a. 20,000

   b. 2000

   c. 200

After Listening

A | Self-Reflection. Form a group with two or three other students. Discuss the questions.

1. Do you think cloning can be dangerous? Explain.

2. If you could clone something, what would it be? Why?

B | Critical Thinking. Discuss the questions with your group.

1. Technology lets us do many things that were once impossible. Can you name one or two ways technology is helping us today?

2. Do you think there should be a limit to what scientists do?

Language Function: Describing Objects Using Adjectives

An adjective is a describing word. It describes *how* something is. Adjectives are used to describe nouns. An adjective does not have a singular or plural form.

Adjectives can come *after* a noun.

Examples:	*The <u>camera</u> is **tiny**.*	The adjective is *tiny*. It describes the camera.
	n. adj.	
	*Amanda's <u>arm</u> is **bionic**.*	The adjective is *bionic*. It describes the arm.
	n. adj.	

Adjectives can also come *before* a noun.

Examples:	*I saw the **tiny** <u>camera</u>.*	*Tiny* is the adjective. It describes the camera.
	adj. n.	
	*Amanda has a **bionic** <u>arm</u>.*	*Bionic* is the adjective. It describes the arm.
	adj. n.	

A | Read and listen to the sentences. <u>Underline</u> the adjectives.

track 2-51

1. The microphone is small.

2. Robots are helpful.

3. Artificial limbs are difficult to use.

4. The scientist is excited.

5. Dinosaurs are extinct.

B | Compare your answers from exercise **A** with a partner. Take turns reading each sentence. Stress the adjectives in each sentence.

C | Work with your partner. Complete the conversations. Fill in each blank with an adjective from the box. Then practice the conversations.

artificial	bionic	interesting	tiny

1. A: The professor's talk was _____.

   B: Yes! I enjoyed his talk about _____ limbs.

2. A: Did you read about the _____ device that helps people communicate?

   B: I did. It is a special computer. It has an

   _____ voice that talks for people who cannot talk.

Grammar: The Future with *Will*

will + basic verb form

We use the future with *will* to express future actions, or when we decide to do something while we are speaking.

Examples: A: *Would you like a cup of tea or coffee?*
B: *I **will have** some coffee, please.*

A: *The lecture is in one hour. Do you want to stay?*
B: *Yes, I **will stay**.*

We use the future with *will* to predict something about the future.

Examples: *Scientists **will make** better robots.*
*Bionic eyes **will help** blind people see.*

A | Fill in each blank. Use *will* and the correct form of the verbs in parentheses.

1. In the future, we will not have farms. Vegetables _____ (grow) from tall buildings.

2. Robots _____ (help) clean the house.

3. Robots _____ (operate) on sick people.

4. In the future, we _____ (travel) by flying cars.

B | Circle the correct answer. Then practice the conversation with a partner. Switch roles.

A: Yesterday I saw a documentary on TV. It was about life in the future.

B: Really? So, how different 1. (is life / will life be) in the future?

A: First of all, we 2. (flying / will fly) places in flying cars.

B: Hmm, OK. That's not bad. What else?

A: Well, robots 3. (were doing / will do) all of our housework. They 4. (clean / will clean), cook, and iron our clothes.

B: Hey, wouldn't that be nice!

A: Yes! And that's not all. There 5. (are / will be) robot doctors!

B: Robot doctors? I don't think I like that. I 6. (never / will never) visit a robot doctor.

A: Well, life in the future 7. (will be / was) much different. But for now, let's enjoy what we have. I say, let's think about the future when it comes!

track **2-52**

C | Read and listen to the article. <u>Underline</u> *will*.

Robots will think, act, and communicate like humans.

Are we ready?

A new group of robots will soon help us in our homes, schools, and offices. According to some robotics professors, in five or ten years, robots will work in human environments. We will watch and communicate with our robots from our computers at work. Some robots may cook for us, fold the clothes, and babysit[2] our children. They will also take care of our elderly[3] parents.

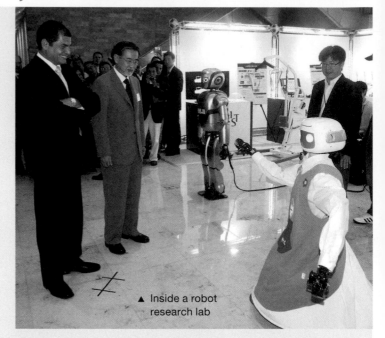

▲ Inside a robot research lab

Here are some good questions many people ask. What will these future robots look like? Will they change the way we communicate with each other? Are we ready for them?

Studies show that people want robots to act like humans. But we don't want them to look like humans! And, we don't want them to make mistakes. Engineers and scientists want to make robots that make us happy. They want to make sure they will help us and make us comfortable. In the future, we don't know if everyone will have a robot at home. But we do know that robots will be a part of our future.

D | Ask a partner questions 1–3. Your partner will give short answers from the information in the article. Then switch roles for questions 4–6.

1. Where will we see robots?

2. How will we communicate with robots?

3. What will robots do for us?

4. When will robots work with us?

5. Do we want robots to look like humans?

6. Do we want robots to act like humans?

E | **Self-Reflection.** Form a group with two or three other students. Discuss the questions.

1. Are you comfortable with the idea of a robot in your home?

2. What jobs will you give a robot to do?

[2] To **babysit** is to take care of someone's children.   [3] **Elderly** means old.

Conducting a Survey

Surveys are important. They collect data or information about how people feel about different topics. You will conduct a survey of your classmates' ideas about technology. Then you will share the information from your survey with a group.

A | Ask three students the survey questions below. Write their answers in the chart.

Survey Questions	Student 1	Student 2	Student 3
1. What technology do you use in your home?			
2. What technology do you use every day?			
3. What is your favorite technology? Why is it your favorite?			
4. Which technology from this unit was very interesting to you?			
5. What technology do you think scientists will invent to make life easier?			

B | **Critical Thinking.** Read the answers from exercise **A**. Think about the information you have. Decide which question you want to talk about.

C | **Presentation.** Form a group with two or three other students. Compare answers. What did you learn from the survey?

> *The most interesting answer I have is for number* _____.
>
> *One student said he/she thought* _____
>
> _____.

Augmented Reality

Before Viewing

A | Discussion. With a partner, discuss the questions below.

1. What do you think the words *augmented reality* mean?
2. What is a smart phone?
3. Why do you think it is called a smart phone?

B | Using a Dictionary. Check (✓) the words you already know. Use a dictionary to help you with any new words.

☐ camera (n.)   ☐ glasses (n.)   ☐ information (n.)   ☐ screen (n.)   ☐ tool (n.)

track **2-53**

C | Read the article about augmented smart phones. Fill in each blank with a word from exercise **B**. Then listen and check your answers.

Augmented Smart Phones

Imagine putting on a pair of (1) _____ and seeing bubbles floating before your eyes! These bubbles are filled with (2) _____ about things you see on the street. This is augmented reality. For many people, augmented reality is already here. It is in their smart phones. Some smart phones have a built-in GPS, compass, and (3) _____. Smart phones can help us find nearby banks and restaurants or the closest subway or bus stop. These smart phones also give us information about other points of interest in some cities. With augmented reality, if you point the phone's camera at a restaurant, you'll see reviews about the restaurant on your (4) _____. Augmented reality is a powerful (5) _____ that has taken us into the world of tomorrow.

D | Predicting Content. Work with a partner. Look at the photo at the bottom of the page. Discuss the question below.

What do you think is special about the eyewear the woman is wearing?

While Viewing

A | Watch the video. With a partner, discuss how augmented reality can help firefighters or pilots.

B | Watch the video again. Complete the sentences with the correct word from the video.

1. On the campus of a New York university, researchers are looking into the _____.

2. This virtual world can give us extra _____ about what we see and hear.

3. This is very good for people going into an _____ that they do not know much about.

4. Imagine if he's successful, you might never get _____ again!

C | Read the statements. Watch the video again. Circle **T** for *true* or **F** for *false*.

1. Professor Feiner is working to augment reality.	**T**	**F**
2. The system allows users to see information about where they are.	**T**	**F**
3. Augmented reality will not be good for tourists.	**T**	**F**
4. Professor Feiner gets lost easily.	**T**	**F**

After Viewing

A | Collaboration. What other information would you like to have about augmented reality? Work with a partner to write three questions you would like to ask Professor Feiner.

B | Discussion. Form a group with two or three other students and discuss the questions below.

1. What surprised you about the video?

2. In what other ways could augmented reality be helpful?

3. In Lesson **B**, you will learn about apartments and farms of the future. Do you think augmented technology will be a part of future apartments and farms?

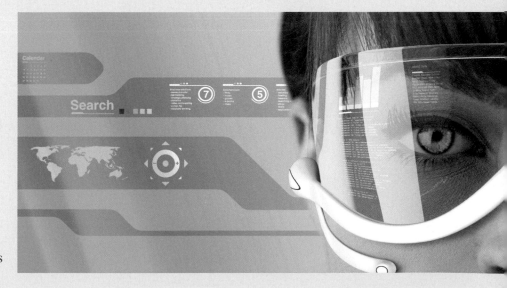

🎧 track **2-54** **Meaning from Context.** Read and listen to the information about three kinds of future farms. Notice the words in **blue**. These are words you will hear and use in Lesson **B**.

FUTURE FARMS

Architect Blake Kurasek wanted to design special apartments. He called them Living Skyscrapers. These future apartments will be special. People will live in them, but there will also be greenhouses[4] in the building. Vegetables and plants will grow inside the greenhouses. Fruit trees will grow on balconies. The ground floor will have a market. Residents will sell the fruit and vegetables they grow in the market.

Another kind of future farm was designed by Italian architects. They wanted to create farms that use seawater. The farms are called Seawater Vertical Farms. They will be high from the ground and will use water from the sea. The seawater will cool and provide water for greenhouses. These farms will be used in dry areas and near the sea. They will be used where there is not enough freshwater or enough vegetables.

The Pyramid Farm is another way we will grow food in the future. The Pyramid Farm will look like a big pyramid. It will grow fruits and vegetables. It will also change sewage[5] into energy for the farm.

[4]**Greenhouses** are buildings covered with glass or plastic for growing plants, vegetables, and flowers.
[5]**Sewage** is waste from homes.

◀ These Supertrees in Singapore are vertical gardens.

A | Fill in each blank with a word in **blue** from page 154. Use each word only once.

1. An Italian _____ designed the Vertical Farms.

2. _____ will live in apartments that have greenhouses.

3. A farm that is above the ground is called a _____ farm.

4. We grow vegetables and fruit on a _____.

5. An architect's job is to _____ buildings.

6. Residents will sell their fruit and vegetables in the _____.

7. In the Pyramid Farm, energy made from the sewage will _____ electricity for the farm.

8. Architects want to _____ farms that can use seawater.

B | **Collaboration.** Using a dictionary, work with a partner to fill in the chart.

Word	Part of Speech	Definition
architect		
create		
design		
farm		
market		
provide		
residents		
vertical		

C | Take turns asking and answering the questions with your partner.

1. What do farmers grow on a farm?

2. Do architects design houses?

3. Will apartment residents grow their own food in the future?

4. Do you think vertical farms are a good idea? Explain.

5. Will greenhouses provide all of our food in the future? Explain.

▲ Vertical farm

D | Read the sentences. Circle the correct word. Check your answers with your partner.

1. A person who designs buildings is called a(n) (resident / architect).

2. (Farms / Markets) of the future will be vertical and placed in dry areas.

3. Italian architects (created / provided) the Seawater Vertical Farm idea.

4. (Residents / Architects) of future apartments will grow their own food.

5. Some future apartments will have (markets / farms) where residents can sell their vegetables.

6. Architects who (design / provide) buildings have very good imaginations.

7. Seawater will (create / provide) water to greenhouses.

8. (Market / Vertical) farms will allow people who live in dry areas or places near the sea to grow their own fruit and vegetables.

track 2-55

Listening for Statements of Opinion

When speakers want to give an opinion, they may use the following expressions:

In my opinion . . .   *I think . . .*
The way I see it . . .   *As far as I'm concerned . . .*
If you want my opinion . . .

Examples: ***In my opinion***, *growing our own vegetables and selling them in a market is a good idea!*

   I think *robots will be very helpful around the house.*

Complete the sentences. Then compare your answers with a partner.

1. In my opinion, Pyramid Farms will be _____.

2. I think future apartments will be _____.

3. If you want my opinion, it is a _____ idea to grow food in our apartments.

Before Listening

Predicting Content. You will hear two friends talking about apartments of the future. With a partner, predict which topic they will NOT talk about. Check (✓) your answer.

☐ Apartments will be special.

☐ People will grow fruits and vegetables in their apartments.

☐ Transportation of the future will be different.

Listening: A Debate between Friends

A | **Listening for Main Ideas.** Read the questions and answer choices. Then listen to the debate and choose the main ideas.

track 2-56

1. Jackie believes _____.

    a. it will be possible to grow vegetables and fruits in apartments

    b. it will not be possible to grow vegetables and fruits in apartments

    c. it is a good idea to grow vegetables and fruits in apartments

2. Angela believes _____.

    a. it will be possible to grow vegetables and fruits in apartments

    b. it will not be possible to grow vegetables and fruits in apartments

    c. it is not a good idea to grow vegetables and fruits in apartments

B | Listening for Details. Read the statements and listen again. Then circle **T** for *true* or **F** for *false*.

1. Angela and Jackie heard the show on the radio.   T   F
2. Angela thought the topic was interesting.   T   F
3. People will grow vegetables and fruits in gardens.   T   F
4. It will be cheaper to grow vegetables and fruits in greenhouses.   T   F
5. There will be fewer people in the future.   T   F

C | Checking Predictions. Look back at the prediction you made in the Before Listening exercise on page 156. Then listen to the debate again. Was your prediction correct?

After Listening

A | Self-Reflection. Think about technology and the future. Rank the following in order of importance (1 = most important; 5 = least important). Then compare your ideas with a partner. Practice using statements of opinion.

_____ flying cars   _____ vertical farms   _____ robots

_____ living skyscrapers   _____ cloning

B | Critical Thinking. Form a group with two or three students. Think about the conversation between Angela and Jackie. Discuss the questions below. Practice using expressions of agreement and disagreement.

1. Is the radio a good place to get information? Is the Internet a good place to get information? Where should people get their information?

2. Do you think people will want to live in apartments where they can grow their own vegetables?

3. Can you think of other ways in which apartments of the future might be different? Explain.

Student to Student

Showing Agreement and Disagreement

In a conversation, you will often want to agree or disagree with someone. Here are some expressions you can use to show agreement or disagreement.

That's right!	*Absolutely!*	*Exactly!*
I agree.	*That's true.*	*I don't agree.*
I don't think so.		

Grammar: The Future with *Be Going To*

am / is / are + going to + basic verb form

We use the future with *be going to* to express future plans or something that a person wants to do in the future.

I am
You are
He / She / It is   } *going to grow.*
We / They are

Examples: *In the future, doctors **are going to grow** body parts in the lab.*

*After college, I **am going to study** to be a doctor.*

*Scientists and technology **are going to change** the way we live.*

  A | Read and listen to the conversation. <u>Underline</u> the future tense with *be going to*.

track 2-57

A: Did you watch TV last night? In the future, people who need a body part are going to get one from labs. Scientists are going to grow body parts from people's cells.[6]

B: What was that again?

A: I said, in the future, scientists are going to grow body parts in the lab!

B: Wow! Really? They are going to grow body parts like ears and eyes in the lab?

A: Yes! Scientists are going to grow body parts that are called bioartificial organs.

B: I guess that will help people who are sick. In the future, if a person needs a heart, liver, or other organ, surgeons will order a bioartificial organ for them!

A: Isn't that amazing? In the future, do you think we are going to live a lot longer than we do today?

B: I don't know. But, I think life is going to be more interesting than it is today!

B | Practice the conversation in exercise **A** with a partner. Then switch roles and practice it again.

◀ A bioartificial ear

[6]**Cells** are the smallest parts of an animal or plant.

C | Write the words in the correct order. Then read the sentences to your partner.

1. vertical / design / Architects / going / are / to / farms

_____

2. grow / is / going / to / parts / scientist / body / The

_____

3. help / are / home / to / Robots / us / at / going

_____

4. to / are / Scientists / going / animals / extinct / clone

_____

5. provide / areas / to / going / are / Vertical / vegetables / in / dry / farms

_____

Critical Thinking Focus

Discussing Pros and Cons

To understand a topic better, you need to think about the pros and cons, or good points and bad points. This reflection will help you talk about the topic on a deeper level. Considering all sides of an issue is an important critical thinking skill.

D | Look at the illustrations. Then complete the conversation below. Choose a word or write your own. Practice reading the conversation with your partner. Then switch roles.

Smart phone   Eyewear   Contact lenses

A: I think smart phones are (fantastic / great / _____).

B: I agree! But, I think eyewear is even (better / more advanced / _____).

A: True. It's amazing that those special glasses can give you information about where you are. Do you think people will really wear them in (the future / a few years / _____)?

B: I don't know. (Many / Some / _____) people may not feel comfortable with that kind of technology.

A: Do you think technology in contact lenses might be (better / more interesting / _____)?

B: I don't know. The world of technology is really changing the way we (live / think / _____)!

E | **Critical Thinking.** Read the conversation in exercise **A** on page 158 again. Complete the chart below. Then compare your answers with a partner.

Topic	Pros	Cons
Write one advantage (pro) and one disadvantage (con) of growing bioartificial organs in a lab.	Bioartificial organs will help people.	Bioartificial organs will take time to grow.

ENGAGE: Participating in a Debate

In this section, you are going to participate in a debate about cloning. First, you must form an opinion on the topic and then plan your debate.

Presentation Skills: Debating

A debate is a well-planned argument. A good debate is supported with facts, statistics, and information. There are many ways to prepare for a debate.

Plan ahead. Research your topic.

Take good notes and learn your material.

Present facts. Use appropriate information.

Be convincing while talking about your topic.

When speaking, stay confident and patient.

Be aware of your body language.

Be respectful. Wait your turn to talk.

Practice, practice, and practice again! Practice makes progress.

A | Planning a Debate. Look at the photo at the bottom of the page. Do you think cloning is a good idea? Fill in the chart.

Pros (Advantages) of Cloning	Cons (Disadvantages) of Cloning

B | Preparing an Argument. Prepare notes using your answers. When possible, start your sentences with the expressions you learned to state an opinion:

In my opinion . . . , I think . . . ,
As far as I'm concerned . . . ,
The way I see it . . . ,
If you want my opinion . . .

C | Debate. Discuss your opinion in a group with two or three students. Listen to the other students in your group. Discuss the different opinions students have.

Dolly, left, the first cloned sheep ▶

Overview

The *Independent Student Handbook* is a resource that you can use at different times during this course. You may want to read the entire handbook at the beginning of the class. It will introduce you to the skills and strategies you will develop and practice throughout the book.

Use the *Independent Student Handbook* throughout the course in the following ways:

Additional Instruction: You can use the handbook to get a little more instruction on a skill that you are learning in the units. The student handbook also includes extra suggestions and strategies. For example, if you are having difficulties following academic lectures, you can refer to the Improving Your Listening Skills section. In the Resources section, you can review signal phrases that will help you to understand the speaker's flow of ideas.

Independent Work: You can use the *Independent Student Handbook* to help you when you are working on your own. For example, if you want to improve your vocabulary, you can follow some of the suggestions in the Building Your Vocabulary section.

Source of Specific Tools: A third way to use the handbook is as a source of specific tools, such as outlines, graphic organizers, and checklists. For example, if you are preparing a presentation, the presentation outline can help you organize your information. Additionally, the presentation checklist will remind you what to do so that you can be an effective speaker.

Table of Contents

Improving Your Listening Skills

Formal Listening Skills	162
Note-Taking Skills	164

Building Your Vocabulary

Vocabulary Learning Tips	165
Dictionary Skills	165

Improving Your Speaking Skills

Everyday Communication	166
Classroom Presentation Skills	167

Resources

Understanding and Using Visuals: Graphic Organizers	168
Reading Maps, Graphs, and Charts	170
Presentation Outline	171
Checklists	171
Summary of Signal Phrases	172

Formal Listening Skills

Predicting

Speakers giving formal talks or lectures usually begin by introducing themselves and then introducing their topic. Listen carefully to the introduction of the topic and try to think about what you will hear.

Strategies

- Use visual information including titles on the board, on slides, or in a PowerPoint® presentation.
- Think about what you already know about the topic.
- Ask questions.
- Listen for specific phrases.

Identifying the Topic:

My topic is . . .   *Today I'm going to talk about . . .*   *Our topic today is . . .*   *Let's look at . . .*

Understanding the Structure of the Presentation

An organized speaker will use certain expressions to introduce you to the important information that will follow.

Introduction

A good introduction identifies the topic and tells how the lecture or presentation will be organized.

Expanding on the Topic:

I'll talk more about . . .   *There are two groups . . .*
There are three reasons . . .

Body

In the body of the lecture, the speaker will give more information about the topic presented in the introduction. The speaker will use phrases that tell you the order of events or subtopics. For example, the speaker may discuss several examples or reasons.

Following the Order of Ideas:

The first/next/final (point) is . . .   *For example, . . .*
First/Next/Finally, let's look at . . .   *Another reason is . . .*

Conclusion

In a conclusion, the speaker often summarizes what was said and may add his/her opinion. Sometimes speakers ask a question to get the audience to think more about the topic.

Concluding:

In conclusion, . . .   *To sum up, . . .*   *In summary, . . .*   *At the end, . . .*

Listening for the Main Idea

It's important to tell the difference between a speaker's main idea and the supporting details. Often a speaker has one main idea and several details that support the main idea.

Strategies

- Listen for the main idea, which is usually at the end of the introduction.
- Listen for questions and then answers.
- Listen for ideas that are repeated or said in a different way.

Repeating/Rephrasing:

I'll say this again . . .   *The most important thing to know is . . .*

Let me repeat . . .   *What you need to know is . . .*

Listening for Details (Examples)

A speaker will often give examples that support a main point. A good example can help you understand and remember the main idea better.

Strategies

- Listen for specific phrases that introduce an example.
- If there are several examples, decide if they all support the same idea.

Giving Examples:

First, . . .   *Second, . . .*   *For example, . . .*   *For instance, . . .*

Understanding Meaning from Context

Speakers may use words that you do not know. Or, you may not understand what they say. In these situations, you can guess at the meaning of a word.

Strategies

- Use context clues to guess the meaning of the word. What did you understand just before or just after the word you didn't understand? What do you think the speaker wants to say?
- Listen for words and phrases that signal a definition or explanation.

Giving Definitions:

. . . which means . . .   *In other words, . . .*

What that means is . . .   *That is, . . .*

Recognizing an Opinion

Speakers often have an opinion about the topic they are discussing.

Strategies

- Listen to the speaker's voice. Does she sound excited or happy?
- Listen for words that signal opinions.

Opinions:

I think . . .   *In my opinion, . . .*

Making Inferences

Sometimes a speaker doesn't say something directly, but instead suggests it. When you reach a conclusion about something that is not directly stated, you make an inference. For example, if the speaker says she grew up in Spain, you might infer that she speaks Spanish.

Strategies

- Notice information that supports your inference. For example, you might remember that the speaker lived in Spain.
- Notice information that does not support your inference. For example, the speaker says she was born in Spain (maybe she speaks Spanish) but moved away when she was two (maybe she doesn't speak Spanish).

Note-Taking Skills

Summarizing

When taking notes, you should write down only the most important ideas of the lecture.

Strategies

- Write only the key words.
- Do not write complete sentences.

Using Notes Effectively

It's important to not only take good notes, but to use them in the most effective way.

Strategies

- Go over your notes after class to review and to add information you might have forgotten to write in class.
- Compare notes with a classmate or study group to make sure you have all the important information.
- Review your notes before the next class.

Vocabulary Learning Tips

Keep a Vocabulary Journal

- If a new word is useful, write it in a special notebook. Write a short definition and a sentence that uses the word.
- Review the words in your vocabulary notebook often.

Use New Words as Often as Possible

- You need to use a new word several times to remember its meaning.

Use Vocabulary Organizers

- Make word maps.

- Make flash cards. Write the new word you want to learn on one side. Write the definition and/or a sample sentence on the other side.

Dictionary Skills

The dictionary listing for a word usually gives the following helpful information:

Synonyms

A *synonym* is a word that means the same thing (e.g., baby–infant). Use synonyms to expand your vocabulary.

Different Meanings of the Same Word

Many words have several meanings and several parts of speech. The sample sentences for a word in a dictionary can help you guess which meaning you need. For example, the word *close* can mean different things. Sample sentences in a dictionary, such as *Please close the door.* and *She is standing close to the door.* will help you choose the correct meaning.

Word Families

Word families are words that have the same stem or base word but have different prefixes or suffixes. For example, the words *safe*, *safer*, *safest*, and *unsafe* are all in the same word family.

Everyday Communication

Useful Phrases for Everyday Communication

It's important to practice speaking English every day with your teacher, your classmates, and people outside of class. Use the phrases in the chart below when talking with others.

Making Small Talk: *Where are you from?* *What do you do?* *What are your hobbies?* *It's cold today, isn't it?*	**Showing Interest:** *That's interesting.* *Really? Why?* *Great!* *Tell me more.*
Asking Questions to Encourage Communication: *How about you?* *What about you?* *What do you think?*	**Giving Opinions:** *I think . . .* *In my opinion, . . .* *Personally . . .*
Expressing Likes and Dislikes: *I like . . .* *I love . . .* *I don't like . . .* *I hate . . .*	**Taking Turns:** *Do you agree?* *What do you think?* *Do you want to say something?* *Your turn.*
Showing Agreement: *That's right!* *I agree!* *Absolutely!* *That's true!* *Exactly!*	**Showing Disagreement:** *I don't agree.* *I don't think so.*
Asking for Repetition: *What?* *What did you say?* *Excuse me?* *Did you say . . .?*	**Asking for Clarification:** *I'm sorry, I didn't understand what you said.* *I'm sorry, could you repeat what you just said?* *What do you mean?* *Could you explain it one more time?*
Expressing Difficulty: *I have a hard time (making a decision).* *I am having a hard time (with this paper).* *It is difficult (giving a presentation).* *It is challenging (working on this project).*	**Encouraging:** *You can do it!* *Don't worry!* *It is fun!* *Try your best!*
Making Suggestions: *Let's . . .* *I recommend . . .* *I suggest . . .*	**Showing Surprise:** *You're kidding!* *Wow!* *That's incredible!*

Classroom Presentation Skills

Useful Phrases for Presentations

Presentations are a big part of classroom practice. Use the phrases in the chart below when presenting.

Introducing Your Group: *Hello. We are Maria, Jen, Tom, and Kathy.* *We want to tell you about . . .*	**Using Graphics:** *This graph shows . . .* *As we can see from this graph . . .*
Giving Examples: *The first example is . . .* *Let me give you an example . . .* *Here is an example of what I mean . . .*	**Checking for Understanding:** *Do you understand?* *Does that make sense?* *Is that clear?*
Asking for Questions: *Are there any questions?* *Do you have any questions?* *We can take your questions now.*	**Concluding Statements:** *In conclusion, . . .* *In summary, . . .*

Useful Tips for Presentations

Remember these tips when making a presentation:

- Be organized—your presentation needs an introduction, a middle, and an end.
- Write key phrases on small, numbered note cards.
- Speak clearly and maintain eye contact.
- Be aware of your body language, facial expressions, posture, and movements.
- Include posters or pictures about your topic.
- Practice your presentation several times.

Remember these tips when making and using notes:

- Use 3x5 or 4x6 index cards.
- Number your index cards.
- Write the main ideas of your presentation, important facts, numbers, dates, etc.
- Write key phrases, not complete sentences.
- When presenting, look at your notes, but don't read them.
- Before you present, practice, practice, and practice again using your notes.

Remember these tips when participating in a debate:

- Plan ahead. Research your topic.
- Take good notes and learn your material.
- Present facts. Use appropriate information.
- Be convincing while talking about your topic.
- Be respectful. Wait your turn to talk.

Understanding and Using Visuals: Graphic Organizers

T-Chart

Purpose

Compare or contrast two things or list aspects or qualities of two things. We often write good things (pros/advantages) on one side and bad things (cons/disadvantages) on the other.

Public Transportation

Pros	Cons
cheap	takes time
good for environment	inconvenient
safe	crowded

Venn Diagram

Purpose

Show differences and similarities between two things, sometimes three. The outer sections show differences.

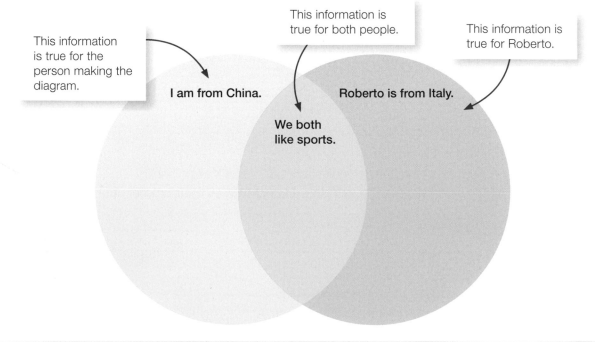

This information is true for the person making the diagram.

This information is true for both people.

This information is true for Roberto.

I am from China.

Roberto is from Italy.

We both like sports.

Charts

Purpose

Organize information about several things. Charts can show information in different groups, different time periods, or different qualities.

Position	Name
Group leader	Maria
Secretary	Tom
Time keeper	Sarah
Presenter	Frank

Spider Map

Purpose

Help organize ideas for brainstorming a topic, planning a presentation, or writing an essay.

Detail
flying cars

Detail
underwater cities

Main Idea
Transportation

Main Idea
Cities

"green" Detail
apartments

Main Idea
Housing

Main Idea
Jobs

Detail
robots do house chores

Topic:
Future Living

Main Idea
Food

Detail
vertical farms in the desert

Time Line

Purpose

Show the order of events and when they happened in time. Time lines start with the oldest point on the left. Time lines are frequently used to show important events in someone's life or in history.

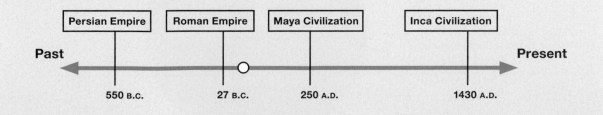

Past

Persian Empire | Roman Empire | Maya Civilization | Inca Civilization

Present

550 B.C. 27 B.C. 250 A.D. 1430 A.D.

Reading Maps, Graphs, and Charts

Maps are used to show geographical information.

The **labels** on a map show important places mentioned in a reading or listening passage.

The **key** or **legend** explains specific information about the map. This legend shows the symbols for capitals and major cities. It also shows how distance is measured on the map.

Bar graphs compare amounts and numbers.

Visitors per year	2008	2009	2010	2011	2012
4,000					
3,000					
2,000					
1,000					

This graph compares the number of visitors each year over five years.

Pie charts show percentages, or something that is made up of several parts.

This section shows that this student's experiences impact 20 percent of his life.

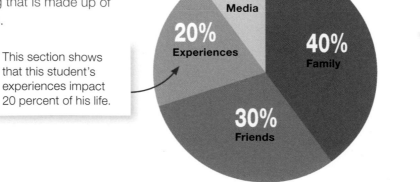

- 10% Media
- 20% Experiences
- 40% Family
- 30% Friends

Presentation Outline

When planning a presentation, you may find it helpful to use an outline.

Introduction

- Topic: _____
- Main idea: _____

Body

- First step/example/reason: _____
- Supporting details: _____
- Second step/example/reason: _____
- Supporting details: _____

Conclusion

- Summary of main ideas: _____
- Closing comment: _____

Checklists

Presentation Checklist

☐ Did I practice several times?
☐ Did I time the presentation?
☐ Do I introduce myself?
☐ Do I maintain eye contact and have good posture?
☐ Do I explain my visuals?
☐ Do I pause sometimes and check for understanding?
☐ Do I use correct pronunciation?
☐ Do I speak loudly so that everyone can hear?

Pair and Group Work Checklist

☐ Do I make eye contact with others?
☐ Do I pay attention when someone else is talking?
☐ Do I make encouraging sounds or comments?
☐ Do I ask for clarification when I don't understand something?
☐ Do I check for understanding?
☐ Do I clarify what I mean?
☐ Do I express agreement and disagreement politely?
☐ Do I make suggestions when helpful?
☐ Do I participate as much as my classmates?
☐ Do I ask my classmates for their ideas?

Summary of Signal Phrases

Identifying the Topic:

My topic is . . .
Today I'm going to talk about . . .
Our topic today is . . .
Let's look at . . .

Expanding on the Topic:

I'll talk more about . . .
There are two groups . . .
There are three reasons . . .

Following the Order of Ideas:

The first/next/final, (point) is . . .
Another reason is . . .
For example, . . .
First/Next/Finally let's look at . . .

Concluding:

In conclusion, . . .
In summary, . . .
To sum up, . . .
At the end, . . .

Repeating/Rephrasing:

I'll say this again . . .
Let me repeat . . .
What you need to know is . . .
The most important thing to know is . . .

Giving Examples:

First, . . .
Second, . . .
For example . . .
For instance . . .

Recognizing Opinions:

I think . . .
In my opinion . . .

Giving Definitions:

. . . which means . . .
In other words, . . .
What that means is . . .
That is . . .

Checking for Understanding:

Do you understand?
Is that clear?
Does that make sense?
Do you know what I mean?

Asking for Questions:

Are there any questions?
Do you have any questions?
We can take your questions now.

accomplishment (n.).......104
act (v.)..........................34
activity (n.)....................114
adapt* (v.)......................94
adventure (n.)..................24
afraid (adj.)...................104
alike (adj.)......................14
ambition (n.)..................104
architect (n.).................154
artifact (n.)...................134
artificial (adj.)...............144
athlete (n.)......................4
attraction (n.)..................74

be a native of (v.).............4
become (v.).....................84
billion (n.)......................14
bionic (adj.)...................144
breathtaking (adj.)...........64

capital (n.)....................124
carefree (adj.)..................4
century (n.)...................124
challenge* (n.)................104
chief (n.).......................134
civilization (n.)...............124
climb (v.)......................104
command (n.)..................144
communicate* (v.)...........144
commute (v.)....................44
competition (n.)................84
control (v.)....................144
convenient (adj.)...............44
create* (v.)....................154
crowded (adj.)..................44
customer (n.)...................94

danger (n.)......................24
design* (v.)....................154
destination (n.)................54
develop (v.).....................84
device* (n.)....................144
discoveries (n.)................34

Earth (n.).......................14
electricity (n.)..................94
emperor (n.)...................124
encourage (v.).................104
energy* (n.).....................94
entertainment (n.)..............84
environment* (n.).............114
equipment* (n.)...............114

estimate* (v.).................134
excavate (v.)...................134
exciting (adj.)..................24
explore (v.).....................34
explorer (n.)....................34
extreme (adj.)...................24

farm (n.).......................154
female (n.)......................14
foreign (adj.)....................4

get around (v.)..................54
get away (v.)....................64
goal* (n.)......................114
gold (n.).......................134

habit (n.).......................94
home country (n.)...............4
hope (v.)........................84

information (n.).................34
inspire (v.)....................104
internal* (adj.)...............124
international (adj.)..............4

lie down (v.)....................54
lifestyle (n.)...................94
limb (n.).......................144

machine (n.).....................54
make a fortune (v.).............34
male (n.)........................14
manmade (adj.)..................74
market (n.).....................154
miles/kilometers
    per hour (n.)...............54
mix (n.).........................74
modern (adj.)....................54

native (adj.)...................134
natural (adj.)...................74
needs (n.).......................34

obstacle (n.)...................114
old-fashioned (adj.)............54
one of a kind (adj.)............14
outgoing (adj.)..................4
overlook (v.)....................74

passenger (n.)...................44
pedestrian (n.)..................44
popular (adj.)...................24
practice (v.)....................84
professional* (adj.).........104
provide (v.)....................154

realize (v.)....................114
recommend (v.)..................74
relax* (v.)......................64
residents* (n.)................154
resources* (n.)................124
risky (adj.).....................24
rule (n.)........................94

safe (adj.)......................44
satisfy (v.).....................34
secluded (adj.)..................64
seek* (v.).......................24
share (v.).......................44
shortage (n.)....................94
signal (n.).....................144
site* (n.)......................134
skill (n.).......................84
sled (n.).......................114
special (adj.)...................14
spectacular (adj.)..............74
spot (n.)........................64

take it easy (v.)...............54
temple (n.).....................124
thrill (n.)......................24
traveler (n.).....................4
treasure (n.)...................134
typical (adj.)...................14

unknown (adj.)..................64
unusual (adj.)...................64

vacation (n.)....................64
valuable (adj.).................124
vehicle* (n.)....................44
vertical (adj.).................154
view (n.)........................74

young (adj.).....................84

*These words are on the Academic Word List (AWL). The AWL is a list of the 570 highest-frequency academic word families that regularly appear in academic texts. The AWL was compiled by researcher Averil Coxhead based on her analysis of a 3.5 million word corpus (Coxhead, 2000).

ACADEMIC LITERACY SKILLS INDEX

Critical Thinking

analyzing information, 1, 2–3, 12, 15, 16, 21, 22–23, 27, 28, 41, 42–43, 49, 56, 58, 61, 62–63, 66, 67, 68, 69, 71, 76, 81, 82–83, 90, 101, 102–103, 115, 119, 121, 122–123, 130, 135, 141, 142–143, 144, 147, 151

applying prior knowledge, 52, 66, 72, 117, 126, 132, 146

brainstorming, 60

checking predictions, 7, 26, 33, 73, 76

comparing/contrasting, 11, 31, 89, 90

choosing the best idea, 51

choosing the best vacation, 71

creating a dialog, 140

describing
- people, 19
- places, 70

discussing pros and cons, 159

expressing ideas and opinions, 15, 17, 27, 37, 97

explaining directions, 47

identifying pros and cons, 55, 57, 79, 159

inferring meaning from context, 7, 27, 37, 47, 56, 67, 76, 87, 97, 106, 117, 126, 147, 156

giving reasons, 12, 13, 23, 33, 138

listening for numbers, 133

listening for order, 46

making inferences, 77, 107, 118, 129

making a list, 59

ordering steps in a process, 58–59

organizing details, 60

organizing ideas, 100, 120

predicting content, 7, 12, 26, 32, 36, 52, 72, 76, 86, 106, 136, 152, 156

ranking information, 35, 45, 157

recalling facts, 139

reflecting, 15

self-reflection, 10, 20, 33, 80, 87, 90, 107, 111, 117, 120, 127, 131, 135, 145, 147, 150, 157

showing agreement and disagreement, 157

synthesizing information, 13, 50

understanding visuals
- bar graphs, 42–43, 57
- charts, 60
- maps, 2–3, 66, 132–133
- pie charts, 20
- timelines, 122–123, 131

understanding main ideas/key concepts, 7, 27, 37, 47, 56, 67, 76, 87, 97, 106, 117, 126, 147, 156

using a graphic organizer
- chart, 10, 11, 13, 27, 29, 32, 55, 60, 71, 72, 75, 77, 79, 91, 107, 117, 150, 155, 159
- mind map, 72
- pie chart, 80
- Venn diagram, 11, 12

using new vocabulary, 5, 15, 25, 35, 45, 55, 65, 75, 85, 95, 105, 115, 125, 135, 145, 155

using visuals to activate prior knowledge, 66

Grammar

the conjunction *because*, 138–139

informational past tense questions, 128

like to, *want to*, and *need to*, 58–59

there is, *there are*, *there was*, and *there were*, 48–49

verbs
- future with *be going to*, 158–159
- future with *be*, 149
- irregular past tense, 109
- present continuous, 68–69
- present continuous in questions, 78–79
- simple past tense, 88–89, 119
- simple past tense of *be*, 9–10
- simple past tense vs. simple past tense of *be*, 99
- simple present tense, 28–29

- simple present tense of *be*, 9

- simple present tense with *Wh-* questions, 38

Wh- questions with *be*, 18–19

Language Function

See also Grammar; Pronunciation;
Speaking

asking for repetition, 69

asking questions to encourage communication, 49

describing objects using adjectives, 148

encouraging, 59

expressing difficulty with something, 108

expressing past facts and generalizations with *used to*, 129

making small talk, 8

past tense time expressions, 89

showing interest, 39

Listening

See also Pronunciation

to articles, 4, 24, 34, 84, 85, 94, 104, 152, 111, 114, 124, 130, 134, 138, 150, 154

asking questions and, 96

checking predictions, 7, 26, 37, 76, 87, 106, 137, 157

to conversations, 8, 9, 17, 56–57, 70, 76, 88, 96, 99, 105, 117, 125, 136, 138, 158

to debates between friends, 156

to descriptions, 6, 44, 64, 74, 89, 112

for details, 7, 17, 27, 37, 47, 57, 67, 77, 87, 97, 106, 117, 126, 136, 147, 157

to directions, 46

for emphasized words, 136

to guided tours, 126

to lectures, 7, 87, 98

for main ideas, 7, 27, 37, 47, 56, 67, 76, 87, 97, 106, 117, 126, 147, 156

note-taking and, 137

for order, 46

predicting content, 7, 26, 36, 76, 86, 106, 136, 152, 156

to presentations, 14, 67, 106

to radio shows, 27

to scientific talks, 147

to sentences, 119, 144, 148

to short documentaries, 97

to short stories, 110

for statements of opinion, 156

to telephone conversations, 78

Presentations

planning, 20, 40, 60, 80, 100, 120, 160

practicing, 20, 40, 60, 80, 100, 120, 160

individual, 20, 80, 100

group, 11, 40, 50, 60, 71, 151

skills

- asking for questions, 40

- debating, 160

- introducing your group, 60

- making eye contact, 20

- presenting to a small group, 100

- using body language, 140

- using graphs, 80

- using notes, 120

ACADEMIC LITERACY SKILLS INDEX

Pronunciation

contractions with *will*, 146

intonation of *wh-* questions, 96

reduction of *-ing,* 77

simple past tense of *-ed* endings, 107, 116

there is and *there are*, 46

third person singular, 30

using intonation to ask for something or make a request, 86

word stress, 6, 127

Speaking

See also Language Function; Presentations; Pronunciation

asking and answering questions, 30, 50, 91, 92, 95, 107, 109, 128, 130, 131, 133, 138, 150, 155

asking for clarification, 139

choosing the best idea and, 51

choosing the best vacation and, 71

collaboration, 51, 71, 77, 108, 153, 155

conducting a survey, 7, 11, 151

conversations, 8–9, 19, 50, 59, 70, 128, 148, 149

discussing
- a plan, 31
- pros and cons, 159
- traditions, 91

discussion, 5, 6, 11, 14, 15, 17, 25, 27, 29, 31, 35, 45, 55, 57, 65, 67, 73, 75, 85, 90, 98, 99, 107, 109, 110, 111, 115, 118, 125, 127, 131, 137, 139, 147, 152, 157

getting someone's attention and, 19

making eye contact and, 39

note-taking and, 139

role-playing, 79, 107, 115, 138, 140

saying thanks, 59

taking turns and, 109

talking about the past, 111, 131

working together and, 79

Test-Taking Skills

categorizing, 32, 33, 54, 57, 70, 72, 75, 79, 116, 159, 160

checking correct responses, 4, 7, 26, 30, 87, 93, 106, 113

circling correct responses, 15, 27, 33, 35, 36, 48, 53, 54, 56, 75, 76, 89, 95, 97, 108, 116, 117, 118, 119, 147, 155

filling in blanks, 5, 9, 45, 46, 52, 65, 69, 79, 85, 88, 90, 97, 105, 109, 111, 114, 115, 128, 135, 145

matching, 4, 6, 13, 14, 16, 24, 26, 32, 34, 36, 44, 52, 53, 54, 56, 64, 72, 74, 84, 93, 104, 114, 124, 132, 134, 144, 152, 155

multiple choice, 27, 47, 67, 73, 76, 87, 118, 126, 136, 147, 156

ordering items, 18, 38, 58, 73, 78, 159

ranking items, 35, 45, 157

sentence completion, 10, 15, 25, 32, 36, 48, 68, 94, 95, 99, 108, 113, 119, 125, 128, 129, 133, 137, 138, 140, 145, 153, 156, 159

short answer questions, 6, 8, 10, 11, 12, 18, 28, 49, 50, 59, 69, 86, 89, 90, 96, 100, 106, 109, 110, 111, 112, 113, 117, 120, 129

true/false questions, 13, 33, 47, 66, 76, 93, 97, 107, 113, 133, 153, 157

underlining correct responses, 7, 8, 70, 78, 110, 127, 130, 139, 150, 158

Topics

Enjoy the Ride, 41–60

Facing Challenges, 101–120

Lost and Found, 121–140

A New View, 141–160

Our Changing World, 81–100

Same and Different, 1–20

Taking Risks, 21–40

Unusual Destinations, 61–80

Viewing

dictionary use and, 13, 15

discussion after, 1, 2–3, 13, 16, 21, 22–23, 33, 41, 42–43, 53, 56, 61, 62–63, 76, 79, 81, 82–83, 93, 101, 102–103, 105, 113, 115, 119, 121, 122–123, 129, 130, 133, 135, 141, 142–143, 153

discussion before, 12, 112, 132, 152

of graphic/visual organizers
- bar graphs, 42–43, 57
- charts, 60
- maps, 2–3, 66, 132–133
- pie charts, 20
- timelines, 122–123, 131

of illustrations, 129, 159

of photos, 1, 2–3, 10, 16, 21, 22–23, 28, 41, 42–43, 49, 56, 58, 61, 62–63, 66, 68, 69, 71, 76, 81, 82–83, 89, 90, 101, 102–103, 115, 119, 121, 122–123, 130, 135, 141, 142–143, 144

of video
- *Antarctic Challenge,* 112–113
- *Augmented Reality,* 152–153
- *Blue Lagoon,* 72–73
- *Coming of Age,* 12–13
- *Highlining Yosemite Falls,* 32–33
- *Indian Railways,* 52–62
- *The Lost World of Angkor,* 132–133
- *Pow-Wows,* 92–93

Visual Literacy

understanding visuals
- bar graphs, 42–43, 57
- charts, 60
- maps, 2–3, 66, 132–133
- pie charts, 20
- timelines, 122–123, 131

using a graphic organizer
- chart, 10, 11, 13, 27, 29, 32, 55, 60, 71, 72, 75, 77, 79, 91, 107, 117, 150, 155, 159
- mind map, 72
- pie chart, 80
- Venn diagram, 11, 12

using visuals to activate prior knowledge, 66

Vocabulary

building
- dictionary use, 4, 24, 44, 54, 64, 84, 94, 104, 114, 124, 134
- meaning from context, 4, 14, 24, 34, 44, 54, 64, 74, 84, 94, 104, 124, 134, 144, 154

dictionary use, 6, 13, 16, 26, 32, 36, 56, 72, 93, 132, 138, 152, 155

using, 5, 15, 25, 35, 45, 55, 65, 75, 85, 95, 105, 115, 125, 135, 145, 155

using prior knowledge, 4, 14, 56

Writing

captions for photos, 68

descriptions, 71

graphic organizers
- chart, 10, 11, 13, 27, 29, 32, 55, 60, 71, 72, 75, 77, 79, 91, 107, 117, 150, 155, 159
- mind map, 72
- pie chart, 80
- Venn diagram, 11, 12

note taking and, 137, 139

presentation notes, 100, 120, 160

Credits

continued from p. xvi

87: Maggie Steber/National Geographic, **88:** Tino Soriano/National Geographic, **89:** KEENPRESS, **89:** Richard Nowitz/National Geographic, **90:** Paul Macleod/National Geographic, **91:** Lonely Planet/Getty Images, **92:** Paul Chesley/National Geographic, **94:** Asianet-Pakistan/Alamy, **95:** Reza/National Geographic, **97:** Frida Gruffman/National Geographic My Shot/National Geographic, **98:** David Yoder/National Geographic, **99:** James Forte/National Geographic, **101:** Michael Nichols/National Geographic, **102:** John Burcham/National Geographic, **102–103:** Gonzalez, Luis/National Geographic, **103:** Tojy George/National Geographic My Shot/National Geographic, **103:** Nick Norman/National Geographic, **104:** Didrik Johnck/Corbis, **105:** Robert F. Sisson and Donald Mcbain/National Geographic, **106:** Photos 12/Alamy, **108:** Justin Guariglia/National Geographic, **110:** A.F. Archive/Alamy Limited, **111:** AP Photo/Ng Han Guan, **112:** Ralph Lee Hopkins/National Geographic, **113:** Gordon Wiltsie/National Geographic, **114:** Cameron Lawson/National Geographic, **115:** Danny Daniels/Photolibrary/Getty Images, **115:** Historical/Corbis, **117:** Pete Ryan/National Geographic, **117:** James L. Stanfield/National Geographic, **119:** Byelikova Oksana/Shutterstock, **119:** Tim Rock/WaterFrame/Age Fotostock, **119:** Digital Vision/Thinkstock, **121:** Kenneth Garrett/National Geographic, **122:** Steve Mccurry/National Geographic, **122:** Victor R. Boswell, JR/National Geographic, **122–123:** Kenneth Garrett/National Geographic, **123:** James L. Stanfield/National Geographic, **123:** Otis Imboden/National Geographic, **124:** Scott S. Warren/National Geographic, **125:** Scott S. Warren/National Geographic, **126:** www.BibleLandPictures.com/Alamy, **126:** Simon Norfolk/National Geographic, **127:** Richard Nowitz/National Geographic, **128:** AP Photo/Ben Curtis, **129:** H.M. Herget/National Geographic, **130:** Michael S. Lewis/National Geographic, **131:** Michael Hampshire/National Geographic, **131:** Simon Norfolk/National Geographic, **131:** Louis S. Glanzman/National Geographic, **131:** Mike Theiss/National Geographic, **133:** Paul Chesley/National Geographic, **134:** AP Photos, **135:** Ken Gillespie Photography/Alamy, **137:** Patricia Hofmeester/Shutterstock.com, **138:** Hiram Bingham/National Geographic, **139:** jokerproduction/iStockphoto.com, **140:** Richard Nowitz/National Geographic, **141:** Christian Darkin/Alamy, **142–143:** Mark Thiessen/National Geographic, **143:** Bruce Dale/National Geographic, **143:** U.S. Gov't Navy/National Geographic, **143:** Jim Richardson/National Geographic, **144:** Mark Thiessen/National Geographic, **144:** Mark Thiessen/National Geographic, **144:** Mark Thiessen/National Geographic, **145:** Mark Thiessen/National Geographic, **147:** Richard Nowitz/National Geographic, **149:** UNIMEDIA/SIPA/Newscom, **149:** UNIMEDIA/SIPA/Newscom, **150:** Kim Hee-Chul/epa/Corbis, **152:** Getty Images Inc/National Geographic, **153:** sellingpix/Shutterstock.com, **154:** Wong Maye-E/AP/Corbis, **155:** Andrea Jones/Alamy, **156–157:** Archipoch/Shutterstock.com, **158:** Shawn Hempel/Shutterstock.com, **159:** National Geographic Maps, **160:** Karen Kasmauski/National Geographic

Maps and Graphs

2–3, **52**, **66**, **112**, **122–123**, **132**, **170:** All National Geographic Maps